HOW TO INVEST IN THE STOCK MARKET FROM PRISON

ELIJAH R. FREEMAN

URBAN AINT DEAD

Email: urbanaintdead@gmail.com

Print ISBN: 979-8-9906748-6-8

CONTENTS

STAY UP TO DATE

To stay up to date on new releases, plus get information on
contests, sneak peaks and more,
Click the link below...
https://mailchi.mp/6d21003686d1/subscribe

Soundtracks

Scan the QR Code below to listen to the Soundtracks/Singles of some of your favorite U.A.D titles:

Don't have Spotify or Apple Music?
No Sweat!
Visit your choice streaming platform and search URBAN AINT DEAD.

Currently on lock serving a bid?
JPay, iHeartRadio, WHATEVER!
We got you covered.

Simply log into your facility's kiosk or tablet, go to music and search URBAN AINT DEAD.

URBAN AINT DEAD

Like & Follow us on social media:
FB - URBAN AINT DEAD
IG: @uadpresents
Tik Tok - @uadpresents

Submissions

Submit the first three chapters of your completed manuscript to urbanaintdead@gmail.com, subject line: Your book's title. The manuscript must be in a .doc file and sent as an attachment. The document should be in Times New Roman, double-spaced, and in size 12 font. Also, provide your synopsis and full contact information. If sending multiple submissions, they must each be in a separate email. Have a story but no way to submit it electronically? You can still submit to URBAN AINT DEAD. Send in the first three chapters, written or typed, of your completed manuscript to:

URBAN AINT DEAD
P.O Box 448
Maybrook, NY 12543

DO NOT send original manuscript. Must be a duplicate.
Provide your synopsis and a cover letter containing your full contact information.
Thanks for considering URBAN AINT DEAD.

DISCLAIMER

The information contained in this book, *How To Invest In The Stock Market From Prison*, is provided for educational and informational purposes only and should not be construed as financial, investment, legal, or other professional advice. The content is based on personal research, experiences, and perspectives and is intended to offer knowledge and insights about stock market investing.

Readers are strongly advised to perform their own research and seek professional guidance before making any investment decisions. The author, publisher, and any affiliates do not guarantee the accuracy, completeness, or reliability of the information presented and expressly disclaim any and all liability for any losses, damages, or consequences that may arise from any person acting on, or refraining from acting on, any information contained in this book.

Investing in the stock market involves substantial risks, including the potential loss of principal. Past performance is not indicative of future results. Ensure that any investments made align with your individual risk tolerance, financial situation, and investment goals.

By reading and utilizing the information in this book, you acknowledge and agree that the author, publisher, and any associated entities are not responsible for any outcomes related to your investment strategies and decisions.

Always consult with a qualified financial advisor or professional before making any investment decisions.

This book covers a wide range of topics related to stock market investing, providing pragmatic guidance, insights, and strategies for incarcerated individuals to engage in the financial markets effectively and responsibly. It aims to empower readers to navigate the complexities of investing and make informed decisions... even from a prison cell.

Welcome to *How To Invest In The Stock Market From Prison*, a unique guide designed specifically for those who find themselves behind the wall but determined to secure the bag. Whether you're new to investing or already have experience in the stock market, this book aims to provide you with the tools, knowledge, and strategies necessary to grow your wealth while incarcerated. In other words, it's gone get you right.

Investing in the stock market from prison might seem impossible but understand that *impossible* is just a BIG word thrown around by small people who find it easier to live in a world they've been given rather than explore the power they have to change it. Limited access to technology, restricted communication, and the challenges of the prison environment can make this one hell of a mission. However, with determination, resourcefulness, and the right guidance, you can beat the system, side-step the obstacles, and make informed investment decisions.

In this guide, we'll address the unique challenges you face and provide solutions to help you overcome them. We'll start by laying the foundational knowledge needed to understand the stock market, including basic terminology, key concepts, and the different types of investments available. Then, we'll get into more advanced strategies, helping you to assess risks, analyze market trends, and build a diversified portfolio that aligns with your financial goals.

I know staying informed and connected is easier said than done, so we'll chop it up about ways to gather information, leverage available resources, and maintain contact with trusted individuals who can assist with your investment activities. Additionally, we'll explore the ethical and legal considerations to ensure that your investments are conducted within the boundaries of the law.

Furthermore, this guide will provide insights into how to manage and safeguard your investments, even when you have limited direct access. I'll share tips on choosing reliable intermediaries, setting up communication channels, and developing contingency plans to protect your financial interests.

Remember, investing in the stock market is a marathon, not a sprint. It requires patience, discipline, and an unwavering commitment to your financial education and growth. While the prison environment adds layers of complexity, it also offers an opportunity to focus intensely on learning and strategy without the distractions of daily life outside. This is one of those things that we have to our advantage. We don't have to worry about bills, clothing, where our next meal is coming from, and a lot of other free world issues. Yeah, some of us help our people with a lot of these things despite our situation because we've been blessed enough to have figured out how to do so, but the vast majority of us don't have these responsibilities. Therefore, we can more easily narrow our focus and turn what was meant to be bad for us into a positive and rewarding situation.

By adhering to the principles and methods outlined in this guide, you can take meaningful steps toward financial independence and create a prosperous future for yourself and your loved ones. Your journey may be challenging, but if you stay down, success is within your reach. Let's embark on this journey together and transform your time into an opportunity for financial empowerment.

Why Invest from Prison?

"Someone's sitting in the shade today because someone planted a tree a long time ago."
Warren Buffett

The stock market offers a powerful opportunity for long-term wealth creation. While your physical freedom may be limited, your financial future doesn't have to be. By learning to invest wisely, you can build a nest egg that provides security for you and your loved ones upon your release. Additionally, engaging in financial activities can offer a sense of purpose, intellectual stimulation, and a positive focus during your time in prison.

I see guys everyday spend their time getting high. Some do their time on the bullshit, in and out the hole. Others...

they're just existing. I think the real question here is are you gonna do time or let it do you?

I don't want to have to ask nobody for anything when I come home. I don't want to be playing catch up with the world when I get out. I don't want to touchdown and have to depend on a woman to take care of me that can kick me out when she gets mad.

If there's one thing that doing time has made me despise is having to depend on people. Being incarcerated means you'll always be dependent on someone for something, even if you're paying them to do it or if you have your own money to get it done. You depend on your family to put money on your books, so you can make commissary (even if it's your money). You need them to order your packages. If you want books (some prisons), your people have to ship them directly from the publisher for you. The list goes on and on, and it can be a real headache when the person you're depending on isn't reliable.

And if that wasn't bad enough, it's even worse when you go to the hole. It's like being locked up all over again. Now, you have to depend on the orderly and officer. You need them to run ice call, you need them to bring you your trays, you need them to pass stuff, and God forbid your toilet is leaking or won't flush. Now, you need them to call maintenance cause your toilet is flooding, and you and your bunkmate have to smell each other's shit. If the orderly or officer are dependable, it'll be handled right away. If not, your cell is officially a port-a-potty. In my experience, more times than not, people aren't dependable. It's hard to find good help. But what if I told you the helping hand you've been looking for has been at the end of your own arm this whole time?

Investing from prison is something you can do to prevent this dependency. You're a man/woman. We're grown. The world don't owe us shit. Don't sit around prison fartin' and lookin' stupid then go home with a chip on your shoulder about who didn't show you no love when you was down. That's hoe shit. Show yourself some love.

Your friends and family have kids and responsibilities, and it ain't getting easier out there. Inflation and interest rates are at an all time high, but there is a way to not only beat inflation but grow your wealth at the same time: investing.

The stock market is a bully to inflation.

With that being said, why not invest from prison?

FINANCIAL INDEPENDENCE FOR THE FUTURE

ONE THING YOU GONE HEAR THROUGHOUT YOUR BID IS someone saying, "When I touch down," or "When I get out, I'ma... blah, blah, blah." The thing you and I have in common with them is that we have plans for when we get out. We may be in different developmental stages within our plans, but my point is we do have plans. Me? I want to travel, but I can't do that in any type of way if I have a job, and my boss doesn't allow me to take the requested time off. Well, if I made enough in dividends to take care of my living expenses, I would only have to work if I wanted to. But let's say I could get the time off, I would still need to make enough money to be able to pay for the trip: the flight, the rental, the hotel, the food, clothes, spending money, etc. That's going to take some bread, and you still have your everyday, ever present house-hold bills to worry about. That's just the reality of it.

You want some more reality? Cool. I got some for you. With each year that passes, things are only getting more expensive everywhere. When I got locked up in 2013, the average rent in the U.S. was $953. As of the writing of this book, 2024, the average rent in the U.S. is $2,115. That's a price difference of $1,162. Add to it the inflated price of gas, groceries, and just about everything for sale. News flash! If you don't have any money, the only place you're going is back to work. What's even worse is it seems like the only thing that isn't going up is minimum wage. So, the wealth gap is only getting bigger. You have to take advantage of your financial future now.

That's why I stress that one of the primary reasons to consider investing from prison is the potential to secure financial independence in the future. Upon release, having a well-grown investment portfolio can greatly enhance your ability to transition back into society, providing funds that might be essential for housing, education, or starting your own business. By investing consistently and wisely during your bid, you set the groundwork for a financially stable future. Don't wait. Start from right there where you are with what you have. Time *in* the market is always better than *timing* the market.

Empowerment Through Knowledge

Investing requires learning and staying informed about the financial markets. This process of acquiring knowledge can be empowering, offering mental stimulation and a productive way to use your time. Mastering the intricacies of the stock market not only enhances your financial literacy but also builds confidence, self-discipline, and critical thinking skills... Did I mention it pays?

Connecting With The Outside World

Keeping abreast of market trends and global economic news can serve as a bridge between the confinement of prison and the wider world outside. Engaging with financial markets allows you to stay connected with societal changes and developments. This connection can be a significant psychological boost, reminding you that you are still a part of the larger economic ecosystem.

Generating Passive Income

Investing in dividend-paying stocks or other income-generating assets can create a stream of passive income, which personally is the main reason I even invest in the stock market in the first place. Even while you are incarcerated, you can potentially see returns on your investments, giving you tangible results from your financial activities. This income might help to support your family or to reinvest and grow your portfolio even further. More on this later.

Preparation For A Second Chance

Life post-incarceration can bring many uncertainties, and having a solid financial foundation can make this transition smoother. Investments made while in prison can provide the necessary capital to start anew, embark on entrepreneurial ventures, or further your education. It represents a proactive step toward rebuilding your life and contributing positively to your community.

A Sense Of Accomplishment

PRISON CAN BE A DIFFICULT ENVIRONMENT WHERE TIME SEEMS to drag on, and personal achievements may feel out of reach. However, monitoring the growth of your investments provides a tangible sense of accomplishment. Watching your portfolio grow, even incrementally, can offer a sense of pride and motivation.

Achievements build confidence.

Building A Legacy

INVESTING ISN'T JUST ABOUT PERSONAL GAIN; IT'S ALSO ABOUT creating a legacy. For many, the thought of leaving something valuable for their loved ones can be a powerful motivator. By making wise investments, you can ensure that your family has financial support in the future, regardless of the circumstances of the present.

. . .

ETHICAL AND DIVERSIFIED INVESTMENTS

ONE ASPECT TO CONSIDER IS THAT YOU CAN INVEST IN A WAY that aligns with your values. Ethical investing allows you to support companies and initiatives that you believe in, fostering a positive impact that extends beyond personal gain. Furthermore, diversifying your portfolio across various sectors and asset types reduces risk and can lead to more stable financial growth. ETFs (exchange traded funds) are a great way to do this. There are some that will argue that diversifying your investments is for people who don't know what they're doing. That's just them poppin' their shit. Some of the greatest investors to ever do it invested in ETFs.

All in all, investing from prison is more than just a strategic financial move; it's an avenue to personal growth, empowerment, and future security. By taking steps now to understand and engage with the stock market, you are investing not just in financial assets but in your post-incarceration life, equipping yourself with tools, knowledge, and resources that will serve you long after your time in prison has ended.

NEXT STEPS

. . .

IN THE FOLLOWING CHAPTERS, WE WILL DELVE DEEPER INTO THE specifics of stock market investing, from understanding market basics to executing trades and managing your portfolio. This guide will provide you with the essential knowledge and steps needed to start your investment journey, even from within the confines of prison.

OVERCOMING LIMITATIONS

INVESTING FROM PRISON REQUIRES CREATIVITY AND RELIANCE on external assistance. Here are some key areas where you may need outside help:

- *Communication:* Establishing a trustworthy person on the outside who can act as your intermediary for executing trades and managing your brokerage account (more on this in Chapter 4).
- *Information Access:* Leveraging library resources, newsletters, and financial publications available in the prison system to stay informed about market trends.
- *Financial Education:* Utilizing any educational programs offered within the prison as well as self-study through books and correspondence courses.

. . .

Making It Work

Success in investing from prison hinges on discipline, patience, and a willingness to learn. While you may face obstacles, remember that the principles of sound investing apply universally whether you are on Wall Street or behind prison walls.

As you embark on this journey, keep an open mind and remain adaptable. The strategies and tips provided in this book are designed to help you overcome the specific hurdles you face and make the most of your circumstances.

By taking control of your financial future, you are making a powerful statement about your resilience and determination. I hope that this book serves as a valuable resource and inspires you to achieve your investment goals, no matter where you are.

Welcome to *How To Invest In The Stock Market from Prison*. Your journey to financial empowerment begins here.

Understanding The Basics Of The Stock Market

"Mastering the basics of the stock market is essential to building wealth. Without a solid foundation, it's impossible to make informed decisions and capitalize on opportunities."
Ian Dunlap a.k.a. The Master Investor

What is the Stock Market?

THE *STOCK MARKET* IS A COMPLEX SYSTEM WHERE SHARES OF publicly traded companies are bought and sold. It might seem complicated at first glance but let's break it down into simpler terms.

Think of the stock market as a large marketplace. Instead of vegetables and fruits, this market sells parts of companies, which are known as shares or stocks. When you buy a stock, you're essentially buying a small piece of a company. Imagine it like buying a slice of pizza; you don't own the whole pizza, but you do own a part of it. So, yes, buying stocks in a company makes you part-owner of that company. I own shares of Apple. So, when I call home and halla at my folks on their iPhones, I appreciate them for shopping with me. Instead of blowing money on designer, why not buy shares and own the brand? The luxury clothing brand, Gucci, is owned by its parent company, Kering S.A (KER), which is publicly traded. Buy shares and you are officially part-owner of Gucci. Hugo Boss (BOSS) is a publicly traded company. Buy shares and you're officially part-owner of Hugo. The same with Louis Vuitton, Prada, Montclair, and all the rest. You can own these companies!

Do your research, buy you some shares, and the next time you see someone rocking these brands, you can thank them for shopping with you. You see all these rappers and movie stars buying these designer brands that you can be the owner of. Why not capitalize off their egos versus playing into the trap of trying to emulate them? Emulating them makes you poorer and poorer, while capitalizing off the brands they wear, talk, and rap about will make you rich. It's a no-brainer. But don't just go and start buying up a bunch of designer brands. First, finish this book, and when you're ready to invest, do so intelligently. Never invest in **ANY** company simply because someone says it's a good idea. I don't care who they are. What they eat don't make you shit, and if it all goes bad, **YOU** will be the one eating that loss. Personally, if I'm going to take a loss, I'ma bet on me. What you look like letting the next man fumble your bag? Don't let 'em piss on you and tell you it's raining. I repeat... always **DO YOUR OWN RESEARCH!!** Thank me later.

WHY COMPANIES SELL SHARES?

COMPANIES SELL SHARES TO RAISE MONEY. THEY MIGHT NEED funds to launch a new product, expand their operations, or pay off debt. By selling stocks to the public, they can generate significant capital without having to borrow money from banks.

HOW THE STOCK MARKET WORKS

1. *Stock Exchanges:* Stock markets operate through exchanges. The two most prominent in the United States are the New York Stock Exchange (NYSE) and the NASDAQ. These exchanges provide a platform for buyers and sellers to trade stocks.

2. *Stockbrokers and Brokerages:* Since you can't directly buy and sell shares on an exchange, you need the assistance of a stockbroker – an individual or a brokerage firm that acts as an intermediary. They handle the transaction for you in exchange for a fee or commission. As an incarcerated individual, you would need someone on the outside (a family member or friend) to help set up and manage a brokerage account on your behalf.

3. *Supply and Demand:* The price of a stock is determined by supply and demand. If more people want to buy a stock than sell it, the price goes up. Conversely, if more people want to sell a stock than buy it, the price goes down.

4. *Dividends and Capital Gains:* When you own shares, you can make money in two primary ways:

   ○ *Dividends:* Some companies pay out a portion of their profits to shareholders. These payments, called dividends, are typically made quarterly (every three months), but there are some that pay out monthly (like my favorite stock, Realty Income (O)).

   ○ *Capital Gains:* If the stock price increases compared to the price at which you bought it, you make a profit when you sell. This is also called *equity*.

. . .

RISKS AND REWARDS

INVESTING IN THE STOCK MARKET COMES WITH ITS OWN SET OF risks and rewards. Stocks can be volatile; their prices can fluctuate rapidly, influenced by factors like company performance, economic conditions, and market sentiment. However, over the long term, the stock market has historically provided significant returns compared to other forms of investment.

ESSENTIAL POINTS TO REMEMBER

- *Do Your Research:* Understanding the fundamentals of the companies you're investing in is crucial. While access to real-time information might be limited in prison, you can request books, financial newspapers, and seek assistance from knowledgeable friends and/or family members.
- *Start Small:* It's wise to begin with a modest amount of money until you become more comfortable with the process. Remember, no action is too small. It all adds up over time.

- *Seek Advice:* Reliable financial advisors can offer guidance tailored to your unique circumstances. If you're able to communicate regularly with someone on the outside, it can be incredibly beneficial to get periodic advice from a professional.

KNOWING WHAT THE STOCK MARKET IS AND HOW IT FUNCTIONS is the first step in your investment journey. Always keep learning, stay patient, and build your strategy gradually. Investing is a marathon, not a sprint, and with time, the complexities of the stock market will become clearer.

BRIEF HISTORY OF THE STOCK MARKET

Understanding the stock market's rich history can offer invaluable insights to anyone, even those currently incarcerated, who have the ambition to invest. That said, allow me to guide you through the stock market's origins and its evolution, providing a foundation that will help you understand how the modern market operates and how to navigate it.

ORIGINS OF STOCK TRADING

. . .

THE CONCEPT OF STOCK TRADING CAN BE TRACED BACK TO THE 15th and 16th centuries in Europe. However, the more formalized version of stock trading as we know it today began in Amsterdam. Here's a concise timeline of its earliest roots:

EARLY BEGINNINGS

THE VERY FIRST STOCK EXCHANGE WAS ESTABLISHED IN Amsterdam in 1602. The Dutch East India Company issued shares to the public, allowing the company to raise capital to fund its voyages. These shares were traded among investors, essentially creating the first stock market. This novel method of raising funds was groundbreaking, as it spread the financial risk and rewards amongst a broader group of people.

DEVELOPMENT OF STOCK CERTIFICATES

ORIGINALLY, SHARES WERE REPRESENTED BY HANDWRITTEN certificates. Investors could sell their shares to others by transferring these certificates. The practice of selling and trading shares gradually grew in popularity and complexity over the years, particularly as shareholders sought to see their investments grow.

. . .

THE EVOLUTION OF STOCK EXCHANGES

SINCE THE EARLY DAYS IN AMSTERDAM, STOCK TRADING HAS significantly evolved, with stock exchanges being created worldwide to facilitate the buying and selling of stocks.

ESTABLISHMENT OF MAJOR STOCK EXCHANGES

- *London Stock Exchange:* Founded in 1801, the London Stock Exchange (LSE) became a significant milestone in stock trading. It formalized many of the practices that are still in place today and contributed to the spread of financial markets across the globe.
- *New York Stock Exchange (NYSE):* Established in 1792 under a buttonwood tree on Wall Street, the NYSE quickly grew to become the largest stock exchange in the world. It's characterized by its physical trading floor where traders shout and signal to buy and sell stocks, a practice known as "open outcry."

. . .

Modern Electronic Trading

As technology advanced, so did stock exchanges. By the late 20th century, electronic trading platforms emerged, significantly changing how stocks were bought and sold. Platforms such as NASDAQ, which was founded in 1971, highlighted the shift toward fully automated trading. This digital transformation made stock trading faster, more efficient, and accessible to a larger number of people.

Global Spread and Integration

Today, there are stock exchanges in most countries around the world, interconnected through advanced technology and regulations. This global network allows for virtually seamless trading and investment opportunities across borders.

Practicalities for Aspiring Investors in Prison

. . .

WHILE BEING INCARCERATED PRESENTS SPEED BUMPS, IT'S STILL possible to grasp the principles of the stock market and even invest. Here's what you need to know:

- *Accessing Information:* Libraries in correctional facilities often contain books on investing and financial markets. Make use of these resources to deepen your understanding. Or if your prison library is shitty and outdated (like the ones at all the prisons I've been to), you will have to continue to buy books like this one that you're reading.
- *Using Outside Assistance:* You'll likely need a trusted individual on the outside to execute trades on your behalf. This person could be a family member or a financial advisor. Ensure this relationship is transparent and based on trust (again, more on this later in Chapter 4).
- *Paper Trading:* Some facilities allow access to "paper trading" simulations or educational tools. These can help you practice and understand market movements without risking real money. I've yet to set foot in a prison who offers this, but my research shows that some do... or maybe at some point they did. I'm not sure. All I know is that the vast majority of people who are employed in the justice departments of every state doesn't

expect us to be on this type of stuff anyways. I want y'all to blow their fucking minds.

- *Legal and Institutional Support:* Check the regulations and allowances provided by the correctional institution. Liaise with your case manager or counselor to understand what is permissible in terms of financial activities.

WITH THIS FOUNDATIONAL KNOWLEDGE ABOUT THE HISTORY and evolution of the stock market, you're now prepared to delve deeper into specific investment strategies that can help you build wealth, even from within the walls of a correctional facility.

KEY CONCEPTS TO KNOW

INVESTING IN THE STOCK MARKET CAN SEEM LIKE NAVIGATING A complex maze, but understanding core concepts will help you chart your course. While incarcerated, you might face certain constraints, but knowledge is power, and grasping these foundational ideas is the first step toward smart investing. In this section, I'll break down three critical concepts: Stocks and Shares, Market Indices, and Bull vs. Bear Market.

. . .

STOCKS AND SHARES

STOCKS REPRESENT OWNERSHIP SHARES IN A COMPANY. WHEN you buy a stock, you're essentially purchasing a small piece of that company. Here's how it works:

- *Ownership:* Owning a stock makes you a part-owner of the company. If the company does well, the value of your stock might increase, and you could share in the profits through dividends.
- *Dividends:* These are payments made to shareholders from a company's earnings. Not all companies pay dividends. and the amount varies.
- *Risk and Reward:* Stocks can grow in value, providing financial gains. However, they can also lose value, making them risky. It's important to understand this inherent risk.

TO BUY AND SELL STOCKS, YOU WOULD TYPICALLY NEED TO GO through a brokerage. Since your access to internet and financial services can be limited, you may need outside assistance to manage your brokerage account, such as trusted family or friends.

MARKET INDICES

MARKET INDICES ARE TOOLS THAT MEASURE THE PERFORMANCE of a group of stocks. They serve as benchmarks to gauge the health of different segments of the market. Key indices include:

- *The Dow Jones Industrial Average (DJIA):* This index tracks thirty large, publicly owned companies in the U.S. It's one way to get a snapshot of market trends.
- *S&P 500:* This index includes five hundred of the largest companies listed on stock exchanges in the U.S. It's widely considered one of the best reflections of the U.S. stock market.
- *Nasdaq Composite:* This index includes over three thousand stocks, mainly from the technology sector.

Understanding indices helps you see broader market trends instead of focusing on individual stocks. Tracking these can be done through financial news available via radio,

TV, or newspapers, which you might have access to. Some prisons offer educational programs or subscriptions to financial newspapers that can be invaluable resources.

Bull vs. Bear Market

The terms "bull market" and "bear market" describe the general direction of the stock market, influencing how people feel about investing at different times.

- *Bull Market:* This is when stock prices are rising or expected to rise. It indicates investor confidence and economic growth. Investing during a bull market can lead to high returns, but remember, prices can also be overvalued.
- *Bear Market:* This occurs when stock prices are falling or expected to fall. It reflects pessimism and economic decline. While riskier, bear markets can present opportunities to buy undervalued stocks.

Knowing whether you're in a bull or bear market can

shape your investment strategy. Information on market conditions can be gathered from financial news and reports.

Each of these concepts forms the bedrock of stock market investing. While incarceration might limit your direct access to market participation tools, understanding these key ideas empowers you to make informed decisions and potentially leverage outside help to navigate the investment world. Continue your learning journey with these basics in mind, and you'll be well on your way to becoming an informed investor.

Getting Started With Stock Market Investing

"You don't need to have a lot of money to start investing; you just need a plan and a commitment to stick with it."
The Wallstreet Trapper

Setting Financial Goals

WHEN YOU'RE GETTING STARTED WITH STOCK MARKET investing, one of the first and most crucial steps is to set clear financial goals. Setting financial goals provides a guide on what you aim to achieve and helps in creating a plan to reach those objectives. Since you are currently incarcerated, it's important to understand how to adapt your goals to your unique situation.

. . .

Why Financial Goals Matter

1. *Direction and Purpose:* Clear financial goals give you a sense of direction and purpose. You'll know what you're aiming for and why you're investing in the stock market.
2. *Measuring Success:* Goals enable you to measure your progress and success over time. Whether you aim for short-term gains or long-term wealth, you need benchmarks to track your journey.
3. *Motivation:* Having set goals keeps you motivated. When you can see your progress, however small, it fuels your determination to continue learning and investing.

Types of Financial Goals

1. *Short-Term Goals:* These are objectives you aim to achieve within a year or less. They may include saving up a small amount of money, understanding how the market works, or learning how to read stock reports.

EXAMPLE: I WANT TO SAVE $500 TO INVEST WITHIN THE NEXT twelve months.

2. *Medium-Term Goals:* These goals are typically set for a period of one to five years. They often involve accumulating a more substantial amount of money for investment or mastering a particular investment strategy.

Example: I want to grow my investment portfolio to $5,000 over the next three years.

3. *Long-Term Goals:* These are goals with a timeline beyond five years, often focused on significant financial milestones like retirement or buying a home.

Example: I want to have a retirement fund worth $100,000 in twenty years.

SMART Criteria for Goal-Setting

TO ENSURE YOUR FINANCIAL GOALS ARE EFFECTIVE, CONSIDER setting them based on the SMART criteria:

- *Specific:* Be clear about what you want to achieve.
  - Example: Save $200 each month for investment purposes.
- *Measurable:* Make sure you can track your progress.
  - Example: Track monthly savings to ensure the target amount is reached.
- *Achievable:* Set realistic goals within your current financial limits.
  - Example: Contribute a part of your prison job earnings toward your investment fund.
- *Relevant:* Your goals should align with your broader financial aspirations.
  - Example: Invest in stocks to build long-term wealth.
- *Time-Bound:* Set a deadline to achieve your goals.
  - Example: Save $2,400 for investment by the end of next year.

Steps to Setting Financial Goals

1. *Identify Your Financial Situation:* Understand your current financial status. Note any income from

prison work, savings, or support from family and friends.

2. *Define Your Goals:* Use the SMART criteria to outline your short-, medium-, and long-term goals.

3. *Prioritize Goals:* Determine which goals are most important to you and focus on those first. It's okay to adjust as you learn more about investing and your financial situation changes.

4. *Create an Action Plan:* Develop a step-by-step plan to achieve your goals. This can include saving a certain amount each month, learning about different types of investments, or seeking outside assistance if necessary.

5. *Seek Assistance:* Certain resources or actions may require help from outside. For instance, you might need a family member or friend to set up an investment account on your behalf. Make sure to communicate clearly and specify your needs.

EXAMPLE: ACTION PLAN FOR A SHORT-TERM GOAL

GOAL: SAVE $500 FOR INITIAL INVESTMENTS WITHIN THE NEXT 12 months.

.   .   .

1. *Assess Income Sources:* Evaluate any prison job earnings or support you receive.
2. *Monthly Savings Plan:* Decide to set aside $42 each month ($500 divided in twelve months).
3. *Track Progress:* Keep a record of your savings each month to ensure you are on track.
4. *Seek Family Assistance:* If needed, ask a family member to hold the savings or set up an investment account for you.
5. *Educational Goals:* Spend time reading investment books or articles to prepare for your first investment.

SETTING FINANCIAL GOALS IS A FOUNDATIONAL STEP IN YOUR investment journey. By clearly defining what you want to achieve, you create a roadmap that guides your steps and keeps you focused, even while navigating the challenges of investing from prison.

CREATING AN INVESTMENT STRATEGY

.   .   .

EMBARKING ON YOUR JOURNEY TO STOCK MARKET INVESTING demands more than just enthusiasm; it requires a well-thought-out strategy. Creating an investment strategy is like building a roadmap that will guide your investment decisions and help you navigate the volatile terrain of the stock market. This sub-section will break down the essential steps to create a solid investment strategy, ensuring you are well-prepared to make informed decisions.

First and foremost, it's important to *set your investment goals*. Whether you're aiming for long-term wealth accumulation, saving for retirement, or generating passive income, clear objectives will shape your strategy and help measure your progress. Next, you need to understand your risk tolerance. The stock market can be unpredictable and knowing the level of risk you are comfortable with will help you make balanced decisions that align with your financial goals and peace of mind.

Diversification is another thing too. A lot of us have heard the phrase *never put all your eggs in one basket*. Same rules apply. Diversify your portfolio. That's a common investment strategy. By spreading your investments across different asset classes, sectors, and regions, you reduce the potential impact of a downturn in any single area. This approach helps to manage risks and stabilize returns over time.

Developing a research routine is equally essential. Stay informed about market trends, economic indicators, company performances, and global events that might influence the stock market. Utilize available resources, such as books, financial news, and analysis reports, to deepen your understanding and stay updated.

Another key aspect is *understanding different investment vehicles*. Stocks, bonds, mutual funds, ETFs, and other financial instruments offer various risk-reward profiles. Choosing the right mix of assets, based on your goals and risk tolerance, can significantly influence your investment success.

Lastly, remember that investing is not a *set it and forget it* activity. Regularly review and adjust your portfolio to reflect changes in your objectives, market conditions, and life circumstances. This proactive approach ensures that your investments remain aligned with your goals.

To get you started on the right foot, here are seven examples of investment strategies you can consider:

6. *Value Investing:* Focusing on undervalued stocks that have strong fundamentals.
    1. *Growth Investing:* Targeting companies with potential for significant earnings growth.
    2. *Dividend Investing:* Investing in stocks that regularly pay dividends to generate steady income.
    3. *Index Fund Investing:* Investing in funds that track market indices, providing broad market exposure.

4. *Buy and Hold Investing:* Purchasing stocks with the intention of holding them for a long period.

7. *Sector Rotation:* Shifting investments between sectors based on economic cycles and market trends.

8. *Contrarian Investing:* Going against market trends by buying stocks that are currently out of favor.

Determine Your Investment Goals

The first step in creating an investment strategy is to *define your investment goals*. Are you looking to grow your wealth over time, generate regular income, save for a specific future expense, or all of the above? Knowing your goals will help shape your strategy. Here are some common investment goals:

- *Long-term Growth:* Ideal for those looking to build wealth over many years.
- *Income Generator:* Suitable for those who need regular income from their investments, often retirees.

- *Capital Preservation:* Focuses on protecting the wealth you already have.
- *Specific Future Expenses:* Such as saving for education, property, or starting a business.

ASSESS YOUR RISK TOLERANCE

RISK TOLERANCE IS YOUR ABILITY AND WILLINGNESS TO ENDURE declines in the value of your investments. All investments come with some level of risk, and understanding your risk tolerance is crucial. Generally, younger investors can take on more risk as they have more time to recover from potential losses. If you are risk-averse, you may prefer safer investments like bonds or dividend-paying stocks.

EDUCATION AND RESEARCH

BECAUSE YOU ARE INCARCERATED, ACCESS TO REAL-TIME information and technology might be limited. However, there are still ways to educate yourself about investing. Seek out books, educational courses, and guides on stock market investing. Many correctional facilities offer access to libraries or educational programs that might have resources on investing. Writing to outside experts or utilizing correspondence courses can be another way to increase your knowledge.

DIVERSIFICATION

DIVERSIFICATION IS A KEY PRINCIPLE IN REDUCING RISK. THIS means spreading your investments across various asset classes (stocks, bonds, real estate, etc.) and sectors (technology, healthcare, finance, etc.). The idea is to avoid putting all your eggs in one basket. A well-diversified portfolio can help cushion against losses in any one area.

DECIDE ON INVESTMENT TYPES

THERE ARE DIFFERENT WAYS TO INVEST IN STOCKS, INCLUDING individual stocks, mutual funds, and exchange-traded funds (ETFs). Here is a brief overview:

- *Individual Stocks:* Buying shares of specific companies gives you ownership in that company. This can offer high returns but also comes with higher risk.

- *Mutual Funds:* These are investment vehicles that pool money from multiple investors to invest in a diversified portfolio of stocks, bonds, or other assets. They offer diversification and professional management.
- *ETFs:* Similar to mutual funds but traded like a stock on an exchange, ETFs provide diversification and typically have lower fees.

DETERMINE YOUR BUDGET

HOW MUCH MONEY YOU CAN INVEST WILL IMPACT YOUR CHOICE of investments and your potential returns. Start by determining how much of your income or savings you can allocate toward investing, keeping in mind your living expenses and other financial responsibilities. It's important to only invest money that you can afford to lose, especially when starting out.

DEVELOPING A ROUTINE

. . .

CREATING A CONSISTENT ROUTINE FOR REVIEWING YOUR investments and portfolio is essential. Even though you might not have internet access, maintaining a written record of your investments and periodically reviewing them will help you stay on track. You might also consider having regular correspondence with a trusted financial advisor or family member who can provide updates and insights on your investments.

STAYING INFORMED

WHILE INSIDE, IT MIGHT BE CHALLENGING TO STAY CONSTANTLY updated on market news. However, periodic updates via letters, calls, or scheduled visits with a knowledgeable person outside can prove beneficial. Additionally, make use of any educational opportunities available to you within the prison to deepen your understanding of the stock market.

PATIENCE AND DISCIPLINE

INVESTING IS A LONG-TERM ENDEAVOR, AND SUCCESS OFTEN requires patience and discipline. Regularly contribute to your investments, stay informed, and avoid the temptation to make impulsive decisions based on short-term market fluctuations. Don't get thirsty and go out bad. Over time, a well-considered strategy can yield significant rewards.

By carefully considering these steps and leveraging available resources, you can create an A-I investment strategy that aligns with your financial goals and circumstances. Remember, investing is a journey, and while it may have its challenges, planning and persistence can pave the way to financial growth and stability.

Risk Tolerance Assessment

BEFORE DIVING INTO THE WORLD OF STOCK MARKET INVESTING, it's crucial to understand your own risk tolerance. *Risk tolerance* refers to the degree of variability in investment returns that you are willing to withstand. In simpler terms, it's about how much loss you can handle while still feeling comfortable with your investments.

Understanding your risk tolerance helps ensure that your investments align with your personal financial situation, goals, and psychological comfort. Here's a breakdown of how you can assess your risk tolerance.

I. Self-Reflection on Financial Goals

- *Short-term vs. Long-term:* Think about your financial goals. Are you looking to build wealth over the long term (five years or more), or are you aiming for quicker returns? Long-term goals usually have a higher risk tolerance since you have more time to recover from potential losses.
- *Investment Horizon:* Determine your investment timeline. The longer you can keep your money invested, the more risk you might be able to take since the stock market tends to recover over time.

3. **Emotional Comfort with Risk**

- *Stress and Anxiety Levels:* Consider how comfortable you are with the thought of losing money. High-risk investments can lead to significant gains, but they can also result in substantial losses. If the idea of losing money keeps you up at night, you might have a lower risk tolerance.
- *Past Experiences:* Reflect on any past experiences with financial loss or gain, even outside the stock market. How did you react? Did you take it on the chin, hit the trap, and make it back? Or did you rob the whole dice game? Different circumstances, I know, and I hate to mention dice in the same breath

as the stock market because stocks isn't gambling at all. I only make mention of it now for you to think back on how you handle losses. This can provide insight into your natural comfort level with risk.

4. Financial Situation

- *Current Financial Status:* Assess your financial stability. If you have debts to pay, limited savings, or dependents relying on your income, you may want to take a more conservative approach.
- *Disposable Income:* Consider how much money you have that is not needed for immediate necessities. Only invest money that you can afford to lose without it affecting your daily life.

Simple Risk Tolerance Quiz

UNDERSTANDING YOUR RISK TOLERANCE IS ESSENTIAL FOR making informed investment decisions. Here's a quiz to help you gauge your own risk level:

. . .

1. IF YOUR INVESTMENT DROPS BY TWENTY PERCENT, WHAT would you do?

a) Sell everything immediately

b) Wait and see if it recovers

c) Buy more because prices are low.

2. What is your main financial goal?

a) Preserve capital (low risk).

b) Grow steadily (moderate risk).

c) Grow aggressively (high risk).

3. How would you feel if your investments fluctuated by ten percent in a month?

a) Very anxious and likely to sell.

b) Slightly concerned but wouldn't make any changes.

c) Excited about potential buying opportunities.

4. Over a five-year period, what average annual return would you be comfortable with?

a) Three to five percent with minimal fluctuations.

b) Six to ten percent with moderate fluctuations.

c) Eleven percent or more, accepting significant fluctuations.

5. How much of your total savings are you willing to invest in high-risk opportunities?

a) Less than ten percent.

b) Ten to thirty percent

c) More than thirty percent.

6. When investing, what is your priority?

a) Avoiding losses.

b) Balancing between risk and return.

c) Maximizing potential returns.

7. How long are you willing to stay invested to achieve your financial goals?

a) Less than three years.

b) Three to seven years.

c) More than seven years.

8. Have you ever invested in individual stocks or high-risk funds?

a) No, I prefer guaranteed returns.

b) Occasionally, but only a small amount.

c) Yes, frequently.

9. How do you react to news about market volatility or economic downturns?

a) I panic and consider selling my investments.

b) I pay attention but stick to my plan.

c) I see it as an opportunity to invest more.

10. If you had extra money to invest, where would you likely place it?

a) In a savings account or low-risk bonds.

b) In a diversified mix of stocks and bonds.

c) In high-growth stocks or real estate.

11. How do you respond to investment advisors recommending high-risk opportunities?

a) I decline and ask for safer options.

b) I consider it carefully but prefer moderate-risk opportunities.

c) I am excited and eager to explore the high-risk opportunities.

RISK TOLERANCE RATING:

- Mostly **A** answers: You have a *low risk* tolerance.
- Mostly **B** answers: You have a *moderate risk* tolerance.
- Mostly **C** answers: You have a *high risk* tolerance.

THIS ASSESSMENT CAN HELP GUIDE YOUR INVESTMENT decisions and ensure they align with your comfort level and financial goals. By taking the time to understand your risk tolerance, you lay a solid foundation for making informed investment choices that align with your comfort level and financial goals. Remember, successful investing is not just about the choices you make but also about understanding your own financial psychology and limitations.

IMPORTANCE OF DIVERSIFICATION

. . .

WHEN YOU'RE GETTING STARTED WITH STOCK MARKET investing, especially from a prison cell, it's crucial to understand the principle of diversification. Diversification is like having a backup plan in every aspect of life; it's a strategy that ensures you are not putting all your eggs in one basket. But what does that mean in the context of investing?

WHAT IS DIVERSIFICATION?

DIVERSIFICATION INVOLVES SPREADING YOUR INVESTMENTS across various assets to reduce risk. Imagine you have $1,000 to invest. Instead of putting all $1,000 into one single company's stock, you might divide that money between several different companies, industries, or even types of investments (like stocks, bonds, or mutual funds). This way, if one investment doesn't perform well, the others might provide a safety net, thus reducing the overall risk.

WHY IS IT IMPORTANT?

1. *Risk Management:* No matter how much research you do, the stock market is inherently unpredictable. Diversification lowers your risk

because not everything will fail at once. If one company you invest in goes bankrupt, the impact on your total investment is minimized since you're also invested in other things.

2. *Smoother Returns:* Different assets perform well at different times. By investing in multiple types of assets, you increase the odds of having more consistent returns over time. For example, while tech stocks might be booming, maybe the pharmaceutical industry is not doing so well. Your diversified portfolio balances this out.

3. *Opportunities for Growth:* Different sectors and asset classes have unique growth potentials. By investing in a variety of areas, you open up the possibility of benefiting from gains in multiple sectors, increasing your chances for better returns.

How to Diversify

Given your unique situation, the actual process of diversifying might require some external assistance, either from family members, friends, or a financial advisor. Here's a simplified roadmap:

1. *Identify Different Assets:* Look for a mix of stocks, bonds, and mutual funds. Stocks are shares in individual companies. *Bonds* are loans you give to companies or governments that pay you back with interest. *Mutual funds* pool money from multiple investors to buy a diversified portfolio of stocks and bonds.

2. *Research:* This step involves looking up information about different companies and industries. You may be able to access financial newspapers and magazines through the prison library. Ask your loved ones to print out relevant online articles and send them to you.

3. *Allocate Your Funds:* Decide how much money to put into each asset. For beginners, a balanced mix might look something like fifty percent stocks, thirty percent bonds, and twenty percent mutual funds. Adjust these percentages based on how much you learn and feel comfortable with.

4. *Regular Reviews:* The stock market changes and so should your investments. If possible, periodically reviewing your investment portfolio is crucial. This might mean asking a family member to help you track your investments and adjust them as needed.

5. *Use of ETFs:* Exchange Traded Funds (ETFs) can be a great tool for diversification. They function

like mutual funds but trade on stock exchanges like individual stocks. If you can manage to get outside help for setting up an account, ETFs can simplify diversification since one fund can include hundreds of stocks across different sectors.

Getting Assistance

1. *Financial Advisors:* Some organizations offer pro bono or reduced-fee financial advice to prisoners. Explore these opportunities if you can.
2. *Family and Friends:* Enlist the help of trusted family members or friends to handle the paperwork and online accounts for you.
3. *Educational Resources:* Many prisons offer educational programs. Look for any available courses on finance or investing. Books and articles can provide a wealth of information as well.
4. *Prison Programs:* Check if your facility has any financial literacy programs. Some prisons partner with non-profits to offer workshops on managing money and investing.

. . .

BY INCORPORATING DIVERSIFICATION INTO YOUR INVESTMENT strategy, you not only safeguard your finances but also set the stage for more stable and potentially prosperous investment outcomes. It's a critical step in your journey to becoming a savvy investor, even from behind bars. More on this in Chapter 9.

How to Invest From Prison

"Start where you are, use what you have, and do what you can.
Consistency and patience are key in the stock market."
The Wallstreet Trapper

<u>Finding a Trusted Outside Contact</u>

WHEN YOU'RE INVESTING FROM PRISON, ONE OF THE BIGGEST hurdles you'll face is the need for an *outside contact*. Prison regulations and the realities of confinement mean you won't have direct access to brokerage accounts or the internet. This makes it essential to have someone you can rely on to handle transactions and manage your investments. I should say *trusted* outside contact cause some of y'all be going out bad. Meet a pen pal in a whole other state and have her holding your funds. We ain't got all that going on with our brokerage accounts. I don't care how much you think you can trust them, how much you think y'all in love, NONE OF THAT!! Trusted contacts only. Preferably someone you have "insurance" on. Below, we will break down everything you need to know about finding and trusting this vital outside contact.

Identifying Potential Contacts

Start by identifying the people in your life who might be both willing and capable of helping you. These could include:

- *Family Members:* Parents, siblings, or cousins who you have a good relationship with.
- *Friends:* Close and trusted friends who understand the responsibility they are taking on.
- *Legal Counsel:* If your lawyer has experience in financial matters, they might be a valuable resource.
- *Professional Financial Advisors:* Though they might charge for their services, a professional can offer expertise and reliability.

ASSESSING TRUSTWORTHINESS

NOT EVERYONE YOU KNOW WILL BE IDEAL FOR THIS ROLE. Consider the following qualities to determine if someone is trustworthy:

- *Integrity:* Do they consistently act with honesty and strong moral principles?
- *Reliability:* Can they be depended upon to follow through with commitments and tasks?
- *Discretion:* Will they keep your business private and secure?
- *Financial Literacy:* Do they have a basic understanding of investing and financial matters?

IT'S CRUCIAL TO CHOOSE SOMEONE WHO NOT ONLY HAS YOUR best interests at heart but also has the capability to manage investments effectively.

INFORMED CONSENT

. . .

ONCE YOU'VE IDENTIFIED A POTENTIAL OUTSIDE CONTACT, HAVE an open and honest discussion with them about your plans.

- *Explain Your Goals:* Clearly outline what you hope to achieve with your investments.
- *Outline Responsibilities:* Be explicit about what you will need from them, such as opening a brokerage account, managing transactions, and staying in touch with you.
- *Discuss Compensation:* If you are asking a professional or even a friend, discuss if and how you will compensate them for their time and efforts.

SETTING UP LEGAL STRUCTURES

TO PROVIDE YOUR CONTACT WITH THE LEGAL AUTHORITY TO manage your investments, consider the following:

- *Power of Attorney (POA):* This is a legal document that grants your chosen individual the authority to act on your behalf in financial matters. A POA can be limited to specific activities or broad enough to cover all of your investment needs.

You'll need legal assistance to draft and execute this document.

- *Custodial Accounts:* Similar to POA, custodial accounts can allow your investments to be managed by a trustee until you are able to handle them yourself.

ACCOUNTABILITY AND MONITORING

TO ENSURE YOUR INVESTMENTS ARE BEING MANAGED PROPERLY, set up some checks and balances:

- *Regular Updates:* Request regular updates on account activity and investment performance.
- *Third-Party Audits:* Periodically, have a third party review the management of your account to ensure everything is in order.
- *Documentation:* Keep a paper trail of all transactions and communications for your records.

FINDING *THE RIGHT* OUTSIDE CONTACT IS A CRITICAL STEP IN your journey to invest from prison. By carefully selecting a trustworthy individual, clearly communicating your needs, and setting up appropriate legal and oversight structures, you can create a reliable system that helps you achieve your investment goals. Remember, the key to successful investing from behind bars is building solid, dependable relationships with your outside contact.

ESTABLISHING COMMUNICATION CHANNELS

INVESTING IN THE STOCK MARKET REQUIRES TIMELY ACCESS TO information and the ability to make transactions efficiently. While being incarcerated presents roadblocks, *establishing robust communication channels* is crucial for your success as an investor. In this section, we will explore various ways you can maintain contact with the outside world, ensure you receive relevant information, and execute trading decisions.

1. *USE OF PHONE CALLS*: MOST CORRECTIONAL FACILITIES provide inmates with access to telephones for making outgoing calls. You can leverage this resource by regularly calling a trusted family member, friend, or financial advisor who can act on your behalf.

- *Make a Schedule:* Establish a regular call schedule to discuss market conditions, potential trades, and updates on your portfolio. Consistency helps ensure that you don't miss any critical opportunities or information.
  - *Be Specific:* During these calls, be clear about your instructions. Whether it's buying, selling, or holding stocks, precise communication can prevent misunderstandings.

2. **WRITTEN CORRESPONDENCE**: IF PHONE ACCESS IS LIMITED, written correspondence through letters can be an alternative.

- *Writing Detailed Instructions:* When writing letters, provide detailed instructions and information, including the stock names, ticker symbols, quantities to be traded, and specific price points.
  - *Receiving Information:* Ensure your contact sends timely updates about the stock market, including news articles, stock performance data, and analyses that can help inform your investment decisions.

3. *EMAIL ACCESS:* SOME INSTITUTIONS ALLOW RESTRICTED access to email services. If you have this option, use it to your advantage.

- *Regular Check-ins:* Schedule regular email check-ins with your trusted contact. Emails can facilitate quicker information exchange compared to traditional mail.
  - *Secure Communication:* Discuss with your contact how to maintain the privacy and security of your investment information within the confines of the prison's email system.

4. *DESIGNATING AN OUTSIDE REPRESENTATIVE:* GIVEN THE limited direct access you have to real-time market data and trading platforms, appointing an outside representative is essential.

- *Choosing the Right Person:* This person could be a family member, friend, or a professional financial advisor. Make sure you select someone who understands your investment goals and has the time and inclination to assist you diligently.

    ◦ *Legal Considerations:* Depending on your situation, consider setting up a legal power of attorney to grant your representative the authority to manage your investment accounts. Consult with your lawyer to ensure this is done correctly.

5. *Subscribing to Financial Publications:* You may be able to subscribe to financial newspapers and magazines, which can be mailed directly to the facility.

- *Investing in Knowledge:* Publications like *The Wall Street Journal*, *Barron's*, or *Forbes* can provide you with valuable insights, stock analysis, and market trends.
  - ◦ *Requesting Reports:* Ask your representative to send you regular updates or tailored reports if you're unable to access comprehensive publications.

6. *Online Brokerage Accounts:* Although you may not have direct access to the internet or online trading platforms, understanding how these accounts work can facilitate

more effective communication with your outside representative.

- *Setting Up Accounts:* Your representative can set up and manage online brokerage accounts on your behalf. Ensure they keep you informed about transactions and account activities.
  - *Learning the Basics:* Familiarize yourself with common brokerage terms and functionalities by reading instructional materials sent to you by your representative or obtained through subscriptions.

By proactively establishing and utilizing these communication channels, you can effectively navigate the challenges of investing from prison. Remember that while you face limitations, *disciplined* and *clear communication* can help you achieve your investment goals.

Providing Instructions for Executing Trades

Executing trades in the stock market requires a clear understanding of how trading platforms operate and leveraging external assistance due to the limitations of being incarcerated. Here, I'll provide a step-by-step guide tailored to your unique circumstances.

STEP 1: ESTABLISH COMMUNICATION CHANNELS

Since direct access to trading platforms is not possible from prison, you will need external assistance to execute trades on your behalf. By now, I've said this enough to where I'm pretty sure you get the message. All the same, ensure that you have reliable communication methods set up, such as scheduled phone calls, letters, or approved email services.

ACTION POINTS:

- Identify a trustworthy person willing to help with your trades.
  - Set up a clear and regular communication schedule.
  - Obtain the necessary permissions and approvals from prison authorities to make calls or send emails if such permissions are required.

STEP 2: OPEN A BROKERAGE ACCOUNT

An essential step in investing is having a brokerage account through a financial institution that offers trading services. This account will be the link between your money and the stock market.

ACTION POINTS:

- Instruct your chosen representative to open a brokerage account in your name or, if regulations permit, in their name for your benefit.
- Ensure that all necessary documentation, including identity verification and funding methods, is correctly filled out and submitted.

STEP 3: RESEARCH AND SELECT INVESTMENTS

Even from prison, you can gain knowledge about which stocks or other investment vehicles to trade. Utilize prison libraries for books on investing, subscribe to financial newsletters if possible, and stay updated via any allowed means of communication.

ACTION POINTS:

- Study fundamental and technical analysis to understand how to evaluate stocks.
  - Create a list of potential stocks or funds to invest in based on your research.
  - Communicate your investment choices and reasoning to your representative clearly.

STEP 4: PLACE ORDERS

Once you have decided on your investments, you need to instruct your representative on placing the orders. Most trades are executed electronically, but specific instructions must be clear and concise to avoid misunderstandings.

ACTION POINTS:

- Specify the type of order: market order (buy/sell immediately at current prices) or limit order (buy/sell only at a certain price).
  - Detail the quantity of shares or the amount of money to be invested.
  - Confirm the order details with your representative to ensure they understand.

STEP 5: MONITOR AND MANAGE YOUR INVESTMENTS

Investing is not a one-time action but *an ongoing* process. Regularly monitoring your investments and making necessary adjustments based on market conditions or your financial goals is crucial.

ACTION POINTS:

- Schedule regular check-ins with your representative to review the performance of your investments.
  - Advise on any changes you wish to make, such as selling underperforming stocks or buying more shares of a promising company.
  - Keep records of all transactions and communications for personal tracking and transparency purposes.

SUMMARY

EXECUTING TRADES FROM PRISON INVOLVES A SIGNIFICANT amount of trust and clear communication with an outside helper. By establishing reliable communication channels, opening a brokerage account, conducting thorough research, and providing detailed instructions for trades, you can actively invest in the stock market despite the restrictions of incarceration. Always stay informed and proactive to make the most out of your investments.

MONITORING INVESTMENTS FROM PRISON

ONCE YOU'VE ESTABLISHED YOUR INVESTMENT STRATEGY AND set up the needed accounts with the help of a trusted outside assistant, the next step is to keep track of how your investments are performing. Monitoring your investments from prison may seem challenging, but with careful planning and communication, it can be managed efficiently.

I. CHOOSING A RELIABLE COMMUNICATION METHOD:

The first and foremost step is establishing a reliable line of communication with your assistant. Regular phone calls, letters, or scheduled visitation times can serve as your primary method for discussing your investment portfolio.

- *Phone Calls:* Make a schedule to call your assistant regularly — weekly or bi-weekly is recommended. Use this time to get updates on market trends, stock performance, and any urgent actions that may need to be taken.

- *Letters:* If phone access is limited, exchanging detailed letters can be an effective alternative. Use these letters to provide clear instructions and to receive comprehensive summaries of your portfolio's status.
- *Visitation:* If possible, use visitation times to have in-depth discussions about your investments. Bring any notes or questions you have to make the most of your time together.

2. ORGANIZING REGULAR UPDATES:

Your assistant should provide you with regular updates on your investments. Here's how you can structure these updates:

- *Performance Report:* Request a simple summary of how each stock in your portfolio is performing. Key metrics to track include the stock price, percentage gain or loss, and any relevant market news.

  i. *Market News:* Ask for a brief overview of major market news that could impact your investments. This includes economic

reports, company earnings
announcements, and significant
geopolitical events.
- *Portfolio Adjustments:* Your assistant should
  notify you of any changes recommended by
  your financial advisor, such as buying or
  selling stocks, so you can provide your
  consent.

3. MAINTAINING RECORDS:

Keep a record of all the information shared between you
and your assistant. Create a simple log:

- *Date and Method of Communication:* Write down
  the date and whether the update was through a
  call, letter, or visit.
  - *Summary of Information:* Briefly summarize the
    key points covered in each update.
  - *Your Decisions:* Record any decisions you made
    regarding your investments based on the
    update.

4. UTILIZING TRUST ACCOUNTS:

If your prison allows it, set up a trust account where your assistant can manage funds on your behalf. This adds a layer of security and ensures that your assets are handled according to your wishes.

- *Bank Statements:* Your assistant should send you copies of bank statements showing the transactions made from the trust account for your review.
    - *Transaction Logs:* Maintain a record of all transactions to keep track of how your funds are being used in the stock market.

5. Risk Management:

Regularly discuss risk management strategies with your assistant. This includes:

- *Diversification:* Ensure your investments are spread across different sectors to minimize risk.
    - *Stop-Loss Orders:* Implement stop-loss orders to limit potential losses on certain stocks.
    - *Emergency Funds:* Always keep a portion of your investment capital in liquid assets to cover any sudden needs.

. . .

6. STAYING EDUCATED:

Even from prison, continue educating yourself about the stock market. I know I've said to use prison libraries to find books on investing and stock market strategies, but I do understand that some, maybe even most, of the prison libraries in America and worldwide are some bullshit. The system isn't built to reform you; it's built to trap you mentally and physically. If you want to grow, you have to want it. You have to go get it the same way you got this book... or maybe you lucked up and someone let you read their copy. Okay, now it's time for you to make your own investment in self.

Ask your assistant to go on Amazon and order you some books. I put a list of twenty-five stock market books that will change your life in the back of this book. Order them. Get an in-depth understanding of the market and build off that. Don't be lazy about your future. Take that same enthusiasm you had in the streets, apply it to this market, and don't quit. Have your assistant send you market reports or financial newsletters if allowed. The more informed you are, the better decisions you'll be able to make.

By establishing a robust system of communication and organization, you can effectively monitor your investments from prison. This proactive approach will help you feel more in control of your financial future and make the most out of your stock market endeavors.

Investing In Individual Stocks

"Behind every stock is a company. Find out what it's doing.
Investing without research is like playing poker and never looking
at the cards.
Know what you own and know why you own it."
Peter Lynch

<u>Researching and Selecting Stocks</u>

INVESTING IN INDIVIDUAL STOCKS CAN BE MORE CHALLENGING
than Index Funds and ETFs. However, with the right guidance and resources, researching and selecting the right
stocks to invest in can be both manageable and rewarding.
Since you'll need an outside assistant to act on your behalf,
it's crucial to ensure they understand your investment

strategy and goals. Here's a step-by-step breakdown of the process:

Understanding Stock Research

1. **Know What a Stock Represents:**

- A stock represents ownership in a company. When you buy a share of a stock, you are buying a piece of that company.
- Stocks are influenced by the company's performance, industry trends, and broader economic factors.

2. **Identify Your Investment Goals:**

- Decide whether you're looking for short-term gains or long-term growth.
- Are you interested in stocks that pay dividends, or are you more focused on stocks that may increase significantly in value?

3. Gather Information:

- *Financial News:* Stay informed about current events, company news, and market trends through sources like *The Wall Street Journal*, *Bloomberg*, and financial sections of major newspapers. Encourage your assistant to update you regularly.
- *Company Reports:* Public companies release annual (10-K) and quarterly (10-Q) reports that offer insight into their financial health and future plans.
- *Analyst Reports:* Financial analysts provide professional evaluations of companies and their stocks. These can be accessed through financial websites and brokerage accounts.

CRITERIA FOR SELECTING STOCKS

1. Company Fundamentals:

- *Earnings:* Look at the company's earnings reports to see if they are consistently profitable. Stable and growing earnings are a positive sign.

- *Revenue Growth:* Check if the company's revenue is increasing, indicating growth and market demand.
- *Debt Levels:* Companies with high levels of debt may be riskier investments. Look for a company with manageable debt levels relative to its income.

2. **Valuation:**

- *Price-to-Earnings (P/E) Ratio:* This ratio compares a company's stock price to its earnings per share (EPS). A lower P/E may indicate a stock is undervalued, while a higher P/E could mean it's overvalued.
- *Price-to-Book (P/B) Ratio:* This ratio compares the stock's market value to its book value (assets minus liabilities). A lower P/B can indicate a good investment opportunity.

3. **Industry Position:**

- Consider if the company is a leader in its industry, which might provide a competitive edge.

- Look at the industry trends and future prospects. Growing industries tend to offer better investment potential.

PRACTICAL STEPS TO TAKE

1. **Create a Watchlist:**

- Alongside your assistant, draft a list of companies that meet your criteria.
- Monitor their stock performance over time and stay informed about any news or changes.

3. **Diversify:**

- Avoid putting all your investment in a single stock. Spread your investments across different industries and companies to minimize risk.

3. **Regular Reviews:**

- Schedule regular check-ins with your assistant to review your portfolio's performance and make any necessary adjustments.
- Staying flexible and informed will help you make decisions that align with your investment strategy and changing market conditions.

UTILIZING RESOURCES

1. **Investment Platforms:**

- Use online investment platforms through your assistant. Platforms like ETRADE, TD Ameritrade, and Fidelity offer tools and resources for researching stocks. Newer platforms like Robinhood, Webull, and Moomoo offer commission-free trading.

2. **Educational Resources:**

- Books, podcasts, and online courses can enhance your understanding of stock investing. Some popular books include *The Intelligent Investor* by Benjamin Graham and *One Up On Wall Street* by Peter Lynch.

BY TAKING THESE STEPS, YOU CAN EFFECTIVELY RESEARCH AND select stocks that align with your investment goals, despite the limitations imposed by your environment. Clear communication with your outside assistant is key so ensure they understand your strategy and can act in your best interest. Happy investing!

UNDERSTANDING FINANCIAL STATEMENTS

WHEN IT COMES TO INVESTING IN INDIVIDUAL STOCKS, *understanding financial statements* is crucial. These documents are the language of business and reveal a company's financial health and performance. For those of you who are new to financial jargon, let's break down the essential components of financial statements and why they matter.

THE BALANCE SHEET

. . .

THE *BALANCE SHEET* PROVIDES A SNAPSHOT OF A COMPANY'S financial position at a specific point in time. It consists of three main sections:

1. *Assets:* What the company owns. This includes everything from cash, inventory, and accounts receivable (money owed to the company) to long-term investments and property. Assets are usually categorized as current (short-term) or non-current (long-term).

2. *Liabilities:* What the company owes. This section lists the company's debts and obligations, including loans, accounts payable (money the company owes), and other financial commitments. Like assets, liabilities are categorized into current (due within a year) and long-term (due after a year) liabilities.

3. *Equity:* The owner's claim after all liabilities have been subtracted from assets. This is sometimes referred to as shareholders' equity or owner's equity. It consists of items like retained earnings (profits that have been reinvested in the business) and stock issued to investors.

A FUNDAMENTAL EQUATION TO REMEMBER HERE IS: **ASSETS = Liabilities + Equity.**

THE INCOME STATEMENT

THE INCOME STATEMENT, ALSO KNOWN AS THE PROFIT AND LOSS statement, shows a company's performance over a certain period, typically a quarter or a year. It includes:

1. *Revenue:* The total amount of money generated from sales of goods or services. This is often referred to as the "top line".
2. *Expenses:* The costs incurred to generate revenue. These can include cost of goods sold (direct costs like materials and labor), operating expenses (indirect costs like rent and salaries), and taxes.
3. *Net Income:* Also known as the "bottom line", this is the profit left over after all expenses are subtracted from revenue. A positive net income indicates profitability, while a negative net income signals a loss.

THE CASH FLOW STATEMENT

. . .

THE CASH FLOW STATEMENT DETAILS THE INFLOW AND outflow of cash within a company over a specific period. It is divided into three main sections:

1. *Operating Activities:* Cash generated or used in core business operations, like sales, services, and payments to suppliers and employees.
2. *Investing Activities:* Cash spent on or received from investment-related activities, such as the purchase or sale of assets and investments.
3. *Financing Activities:* Cash obtained from or paid to investors and creditors, including issuing stocks, borrowing money, and repaying debts.

THIS STATEMENT HELPS YOU UNDERSTAND HOW WELL A company manages its cash, which is critical for sustaining operations and growth.

WHY ARE FINANCIAL STATEMENTS IMPORTANT?

. . .

By carefully analyzing these statements, you and your outside assistant can assess a company's:

- *Financial Health:* Determine if the company is financially stable or in trouble.
- *Performance Over Time:* Track growth, profitability, and efficiency trends.
- *Viability as an Investment:* Identify whether the company has potential for long-term success and profitability.

In summary, understanding financial statements allows you to make informed decisions when selecting individual stocks. This knowledge will equip you with the tools to evaluate companies more effectively and increase your chances of building a successful investment portfolio, even from within the confines of prison.

By mastering the basics of financial statements, you're taking a significant step toward becoming a savvy investor. Remember, everyone starts somewhere, and learning these fundamentals will serve as a strong foundation for your investing journey.

· · ·

Evaluating a Company's Performance and Growth Potential

When you're looking to invest in individual stocks, one of the most crucial steps is *evaluating a company's performance and growth potential.* Understanding whether a company is doing well and if it has the potential to grow in the future will help you make informed investment decisions. Let's break it down.

Understanding Financial Statements

To start evaluating a company, you'll need to look at its financial statements. These documents give you a snapshot of the company's financial health. The three main types of financial statements are:

1. *Income Statement:* This shows the company's revenues (how much money it's making), expenses (how much it's spending), and profits (how much it has left after paying all its expenses) over a certain period, usually a quarter (three months) or a year.

2. *Balance Sheet:* This shows what the company owns (assets), what it owes (liabilities), and what is left for the shareholders (equity). Think of it as a snapshot of the company's financial condition at a specific point in time.

3. *Cash Flow Statement:* This highlights how cash is moving in and out of the company. It shows where the company is getting its money from and how it's spending it. This is important because a company needs cash to operate and grow.

SINCE YOU MAY NEED AN OUTSIDE ASSISTANT TO ACCESS AND understand these statements, a family member, friend, or financial advisor could help you obtain them and explain their significance.

KEY FINANCIAL METRICS

ONCE YOU HAVE ACCESS TO THESE FINANCIAL STATEMENTS, you'll need to understand some key metrics that can help you evaluate the company's performance:

1. *Revenue Growth:* This indicates how quickly the company's sales are increasing. Strong revenue growth often signals a growing business.

2. *Profit Margin:* This measures how much profit the company makes for every dollar of sales. It's calculated as Net Income divided by Revenue. Higher margins mean the company is more efficient at converting sales into actual profit.

3. *Earnings Per Share (EPS):* EPS tells you how much profit the company makes for each share of its stock. It's calculated as Net Income divided by the Number of Outstanding Shares. Consistently growing EPS is a good sign of a healthy company.

4. *Return on Equity (ROE):* This measures how well the company is using shareholders' money to generate profit. It's calculated as Net Income divided by Shareholders' Equity. A higher ROE indicates a more effective management team.

QUALITATIVE ANALYSIS

APART FROM THE NUMBERS, IT'S IMPORTANT TO UNDERSTAND the qualitative aspects of the company. This includes:

1. *Management Team:* The company's leaders and their track record. Strong leadership often drives a company's success.

2. *Competitive Advantage:* What sets the company apart from its competitors? This could be a strong brand, patents, exclusive technologies, or a loyal customer base. Warren Buffett famously termed this a company's *moat.*

3. *Industry Position:* How does the company stand in comparison to its competitors? Is it a leader, or is it struggling to keep up?

4. *Market Trends:* Are there upcoming trends that might benefit or hurt the company? For example, tech companies might thrive with the increase in digital transformation, while traditional retail companies might face challenges with the shift to online shopping.

FUTURE GROWTH POTENTIAL

AFTER UNDERSTANDING THE COMPANY'S CURRENT performance, consider its potential for future growth. Here are some things to look for:

1. *Expansion Plans:* Does the company have plans to enter new markets or launch new products? Expansion can drive growth.

2. *Research and Development:* Is the company investing in innovation? High investment in R&D suggests the company is working on future growth products or services.

3. *Market Growth:* Is the industry growing? Investing in a company in a growing market might offer better returns.

4. *Past Performance:* While not always indicative of future results, a company with a history of strong growth is more likely to continue growing.

IN SUMMARY, EVALUATING A COMPANY'S PERFORMANCE AND growth potential involves both a quantitative look at financial metrics and a qualitative assessment of its business position and market context. Utilizing your outside assistant to gather and analyze this information can help you make more informed stock investment decisions, even from within prison.

Exploring Dividend Stocks

"Dividends are an investor's best friend. A steady, growing dividend stream rewards shareholders and aligns business performance with shareholder interests."
Warren Buffett

<u>My Introduction To The Market</u>

THERE CAME A TIME IN MY BID WHERE I WAS IN A DORM THAT was constantly getting our commissary privileges taken on a regular. If administration came and we weren't ready for inspection – no store. Dorm talking in the chow hall – no store. If there was a stabbing and the cameras got covered up – store took. Someone in the dorm stopped at the gate to talk to someone in another dorm on our way to or from the dorm

– over with. You might as well not even think about going to the store, which sucked for me because selling store bags was my number one hustle at the time. There are a lot of people behind the wall that are on store restriction because of write-ups, some owe the state and know that they will only take the money if they have their people add it to their books, and then you have the people that just want extra food. I would max out eight to ten names in commissary and cash them out, giving them fifteen for twenty-five dollars. Which wasn't even a full fifteen dollars because items were rounded to the next dollar where I was at the time. For instance, if a bag of chips was $1.19, the item would be considered $2. If rice was $1.03 at the store, it was considered $2 in a cash out. So, it was a good legal hustle. I would get inmate's name and GDC numbers who couldn't afford to go to store and let them get $15 of the money, but I would go in their names. Sometimes, I would just have my people Cash App their people $25 for them to do whatever they wanted with it, and I would still eat good! It was an AI legal hustle... but the weeks we got our store took hurt me bad.

Then, one day, unfortunately, someone was killed in the dorm I was in, and the cameras had been covered up. The warden dragged us. We didn't get store for a month, and when we were allowed to go, we were only allowed to go for $30 in food and had to slowly work our way back up. I started thinking then about a way to get money regardless of what happened in prison. I was already aware of passive income because I was getting royalty checks for the books I had out. Royalty checks came whether they took the store or not. I needed some more streams of income like that. I called my brother the next day, had him go on YouTube and type in "Passive Income Ideas", and a video popped titled, *50 Passive Income Ideas*. It was in this video that I discovered Dividend Investing.

For the last year and a half, my fiancée had been telling me I should read up on stocks. She felt that, like most things I put my mind to, if I locked in on it, I could master it. I was hearing her, but at the time, I was more focused on figuring out the publishing thing. I looked at a video or two, but the whole stock thing seemed too complicated. *Dividend Investing* was the first concept about the stock market that I could understand. I mean, come on. What was so hard about being paid a certain amount of money monthly, bi-monthly, quarterly, or annually? I thought to myself if I put a little something into a dividend stock weekly, whenever something slowed up or we got our store took, I could still count on money to be coming through. Even better, if you stack your bread in dividend stocks, you'll have another stream of income to depend on when you touch down. Essentially, you want your passive income to be able to take care of your living expenses. So, for example: if your rent, utilities, car note, food, clothes, gas in your car, insurance, and miscellaneous expenses per month are 5K, your job would be to figure out how many shares of a company you would need to own to receive 5K a month in dividends. That way, you don't have to rely on anyone else, and whatever other money you make will be free cash flow for you to do as you please.

But, I won't lie. The amount needed to make this happen will be steep, which is why the sooner you get started, the better. This way, you can get the benefits of compound interest.

From my small cell, I made a plan. It wasn't like I had a nine-to-five to fall back on, so I had to be strategic. I started by reaching out to my family on the outside and getting them to set up the necessary accounts for me. Once the accounts were in place, I instructed my family to send me information on various dividend stocks. I read every piece of material I could get my hands on – books, articles, anything that was available in the library or that could be mailed in.

The journey wasn't easy. I had limited resources, but I was determined. Every bit of my commissary money that I didn't use for absolute essentials, I invested in stocks through my family. Some months, it was just a few dollars, but I knew every bit would count over time.

It's a constant hustle, but by taking it slow and steadily, I saw my investments begin to grow. Watching those dividends get paid out — even if it was just a couple of bucks — felt like a little victory each time. It made me realize that even behind bars, I could still build something meaningful and secure a financial future.

I found a sense of purpose in this. It wasn't just about the money; it was about taking control of my destiny. It gave me something positive to focus on each day, a beacon of hope in a place where hope is hard to come by. Each investment, each earned dividend, was a step closer to financial freedom, a way to ensure that when I'm out, I won't be starting from scratch.

If I could share one piece of advice with anyone else in my situation, it would be this: *don't be discouraged by what you can't do, focus on what you **can**.* Whether you can invest a lot or a little, start where you are. Every small step counts. And who knows? Those small steps might just lead to big changes, even from within these walls.

What Are Dividend Stocks?

IN THE FASCINATING WORLD OF INVESTING, DIVIDEND STOCKS stand out as one of the most attractive options for building and growing wealth, especially for someone doing time. Understanding what dividend stocks are and how they work can provide an AI avenue for generating income and securing financial stability.

Breaking Down Dividends:

. . .

A *DIVIDEND* IS ESSENTIALLY A REWARD THAT A COMPANY PAYS TO its shareholders. When you own a share of a company, you own a tiny piece of that company. As the company earns money, it often decides to share a portion of its profits with its shareholders in the form of dividends. This is typically done on a regular basis, such as quarterly (every three months). But there are some stocks that pay you monthly if you, like myself, prefer that.

EXAMPLE: IMAGINE COMPANY XYZ PERFORMS WELL AND MAKES a profit. If you own shares in Company XYZ, the company may decide to distribute part of its profits to you and its other shareholders. If the dividend is $1 per share and you own ten shares, you would receive $10 in dividends for that period.

1. <u>Types of Dividend Stocks:</u> **Regular Dividend Stocks:**
   - These stocks pay dividends consistently, usually on a quarterly basis. They offer a reliable stream of income, which makes them attractive to investors seeking stability.
2. **High-Yield Dividend Stocks:**
   - These stocks pay higher-than-average dividends. While they offer a mouth-watering

income, they may come with higher risks, such as being in volatile industries.

3. **Dividend Aristocrats:**
   - These are companies that have consistently increased their dividends for at least twenty-five consecutive years. They are considered to be stable and reliable investments.

GETTING STARTED WITH DIVIDEND STOCKS:

1. **Research:**
   - With help from your outside assistant, research companies that pay dividends using reliable financial news websites and resources.
2. **Selection:**
   - Choose companies that have a strong track record of paying and increasing dividends. Look for Dividend Aristocrats if you seek long-term stability.
3. **Buy Shares:**
   - Instruct your outside assistant to purchase shares of these companies on your behalf through a brokerage account. Make sure they reinvest the dividends you earn to buy more

shares, a process known as Dividend Reinvestment Program (DRIP).

Why Choose Dividend Stocks?

1. **Income Generation:**
   - They provide a steady stream of income, which is particularly useful when looking to generate funds while being incarcerated.
2. **Reinvestment Opportunities:**
   - Reinvesting dividends can help grow your investment over time, benefiting from the power of compounding. Compound interest is the gift that keeps on giving. It leads you to accelerating your wealth.
3. **Stability:**
   - Many dividend-paying companies are established and stable, which may help mitigate some risks associated with investing.

Conclusion

Dividend stocks can be a powerful tool in your investment arsenal. By understanding what they are and how they work, you can strategically select investments that provide regular income and potential growth. Remember, consistent research and the guidance of your outside assistant are crucial for making informed decisions and managing your investments wisely.

BENEFITS OF DIVIDEND INVESTING

Dividend investing can be a powerful strategy, especially for those looking to build wealth over time. Even while incarcerated, understanding how dividends work can help you make informed decisions and provide you with a source of income. Let's break down the benefits of investing in dividend stocks in a way that's easy to understand.

REGULAR INCOME

One of the primary benefits of investing in dividend stocks is *the regular income* they provide. When a company earns a profit, it often shares a portion of that profit with its shareholders in the form of dividends. For example, if you own shares of a company that pays quarterly dividends, you can expect to receive a payment every three months. This can be a reliable source of income, especially if you invest in companies with a history of consistent dividends.

Imagine this as receiving a monthly allowance, but

instead of it coming from your family or a job, it's coming from profits made by the companies you've invested in. This dividend income can accumulate over time and reinvested to buy more shares, which can lead to even more dividends in the future.

POTENTIAL FOR GROWTH AND COMPOUNDING

DIVIDENDS CAN DO MORE THAN JUST PROVIDE REGULAR income; they can also contribute to the growth of your investment portfolio. When you reinvest your dividends, you are using those earnings to purchase more shares of the stock. Over time, this process, known as *compounding*, can significantly increase the value of your initial investment.

For example, let's say you own a stock that pays an annual dividend of $1 per share, and you use that $1 to buy more of the same stock. Next year, you'll receive dividends on those additional shares as well, leading to even more dividend payments in the future. As this cycle continues, the value of your investment can grow exponentially.

LOWER RISK

. . .

DIVIDEND-PAYING STOCKS ARE OFTEN ASSOCIATED WITH LOWER risk compared to non-dividend-paying stocks. Companies that regularly pay dividends tend to be established businesses with stable earnings. These companies are often less volatile, meaning their stock prices don't fluctuate as dramatically as those of younger, less established companies.

This stability can make dividend stocks a safer choice, especially for new investors who are still learning the ropes. While no investment is entirely risk-free, dividend-paying stocks can provide a level of security and predictability that can be comforting.

TAX ADVANTAGES

DEPENDING ON YOUR CIRCUMSTANCES, THERE CAN BE TAX advantages to earning income through dividends. In some cases, qualified dividends are taxed at a lower rate than regular income, which can make them a more tax-efficient way to earn money. Be sure to consult with your outside assistant or a tax professional to understand how dividends will be taxed in your specific situation.

INFLATION HEDGE

. . .

LASTLY, DIVIDEND-PAYING STOCKS CAN ACT AS A HEDGE AGAINST inflation. Inflation erodes the purchasing power of money over time, meaning what you can buy with a dollar today will cost more in the future. However, many companies increase their dividend payments over time, helping you keep pace with inflation. This increasing income can help maintain your purchasing power, even as prices rise. As Wallstreet Trapper would say, "The stock market is a bully to inflation." Dividends do the beating.

In summary, the benefits of dividend investing include regular income, the potential for growth and compounding, lower risk, tax advantages, and an inflation hedge. Understanding these benefits can help you make informed decisions and build a solid foundation for your investment portfolio, even from behind bars. Using these insights, you and your outside assistant can work together to identify strong dividend-paying stocks that align with your long-term financial goals.

HOW TO IDENTIFY RELIABLE DIVIDEND PAYING COMPANIES

INVESTING IN DIVIDEND-PAYING STOCKS CAN BE A SMART WAY TO build wealth. Dividends are payments that companies make to their shareholders, usually on a regular basis, such as quarterly. These payments come from the company's profits, and they can provide you with a steady income stream while you own the stock. But not all dividend-paying companies are created equal. Here's a step-by-step guide on how to identify reliable ones:

1. Look at the Dividend History

A reliable dividend-paying company usually has a long track record of paying dividends consistently. Often, such companies not only pay dividends but increase them over time. Here's what you can instruct your outside assistant to do:

- *Research the company's dividend history*: Ask your assistant to look up how long the company has been paying dividends and whether those payments have been consistent or growing. If a company has been paying and raising its dividends for at least ten to twenty years, that's a good sign.

2. CHECK THE DIVIDEND YIELD

The dividend yield is a percentage that indicates how much a company pays out in dividends each year relative to its stock price. Here's the formula:

- Take the total dividends a stock pays you in a year (Annual Dividend Per Share).
  - Divide that amount by the current price of the stock (Stock Price Per Share).
  - Finally, multiply by 100 to get a percentage.

THINK OF IT AS FIGURING OUT WHAT PERCENTAGE OF THE stock's price you get back in a year just from dividends. Remember:

- Higher isn't always better. While a higher dividend yield can seem attractive, yields that are too high might indicate that the company is struggling and using high dividends to lure investors. A dividend yield between two percent and six percent is generally a good range to aim for.

3. EVALUATE FINANCIAL HEALTH

A company's ability to pay and increase dividends depends on its financial health. Here's what your assistant should look for:

- *Revenue and Earnings Growth:* Consistent revenue and profit growth means the company is making more money over time, which is essential for sustaining dividends.
  - *Payout Ratio:* This is the percentage of earnings paid out as dividends. If a company pays too high a percentage of its earnings as dividends, there may be risks. A payout ratio below sixty percent is often considered safe.

4. Strong Cash Flow

Cash flow is the money that comes in and out of a company. A strong and stable cash flow indicates that the company has enough money to pay its bills, reinvest in the business, and pay dividends.

- *Free Cash Flow (FCF):* This is what's left after the company spends money on operations and capital expenditures. Ask your assistant to look for companies with positive and stable free cash flow numbers.

5. Low Debt Levels

High debt can be a warning sign. Companies that are highly leveraged (i.e., have a lot of debt) might struggle to maintain dividend payments during tough times.

- *Debt-to-Equity Ratio:* This metric compares the company's total debt to its shareholder equity. The lower the ratio, the less risky the company is considered to be. A ratio below one is generally seen as favorable.

6. INDUSTRY POSITION

Companies that are leaders in stable and less cyclical industries (i.e., industries that don't go through extreme booms and busts) are often more reliable dividend payers. Sectors like utilities, telecommunications, and consumer staples (everyday essential products) are commonly known for paying steady dividends.

7. MANAGEMENT QUALITY

The quality of a company's management team can significantly affect its long-term viability and ability to pay dividends.

- *Management's track record:* Ask your assistant to find information about the company's management. A stable and experienced management team with a history of prudent financial management can be a huge asset.

By considering these factors and utilizing the help of your outside assistant to gather and analyze information, you can identify companies that are more likely to offer reliable dividend payments. Remember, investing in dividend-paying stocks is a long-term strategy, and it's important to continually monitor your investments to ensure they remain solid choices for your portfolio.

MONTHLY DIVIDEND STOCKS

WHEN EXPLORING DIVIDEND STOCKS, ONE UNIQUE OPTION THAT deserves special attention is *the monthly dividend stock*. Most dividend-paying stocks distribute their earnings to shareholders on a quarterly basis, meaning four times a year. However, monthly dividend stocks do things a little differently. As the name suggests, these stocks pay out dividends every month.

. . .

WHY MONTHLY DIVIDENDS?

THE APPEAL OF MONTHLY DIVIDEND STOCKS LIES PRIMARILY IN the frequency of payouts. Receiving dividends on a monthly basis can help provide more consistent and predictable income. This can be particularly useful if you're relying on your investment returns for regular expenses or if you simply prefer seeing returns more frequently.

HOW TO IDENTIFY MONTHLY DIVIDEND STOCKS

IDENTIFYING MONTHLY DIVIDEND STOCKS INVOLVES A BIT OF research, but with the help of your outside assistant, it's entirely manageable. Follow these steps:

1. *Research and Lists:* Start by conducting research or asking your assistant to find lists of companies that pay dividends monthly. Several financial websites and investment platforms often maintain such lists. Look for keywords like "monthly dividend stocks" or "monthly income stocks."
2. *Company Reputation:* Once you have a list, delve deeper into the company's reputation and financial health. Consistent monthly dividend

payments are a good sign, but you also want to ensure the company has a stable financial footing to sustain those payments. This can involve looking at aspects such as their earnings, payout ratios, and history of dividend payments.

3. *Stock Metrics:* Pay attention to metrics like the dividend yield, which is the ratio of the annual dividend payment to the stock price. This helps you understand how much return you're getting in comparison to the price you've paid for the stock. Ideally, you want a balance between a good yield and a solid company.

Advantages of Monthly Dividend Stocks

- *Steady Income:* Because dividends are paid out monthly, you can enjoy a more regular stream of income, making it easier to budget and plan.

- *Compounding:* Monthly dividends can be reinvested to buy more shares, which can potentially lead to a faster compounding effect compared to quarterly dividends.

. . .

- *Smoothing Out Volatility:* More frequent payouts can help mitigate some of the stock market's volatility. This steady return can act as a cushion against the ups and downs of stock prices.

Popular Monthly Dividend Stocks

Here are a few examples of companies and funds known for paying monthly dividends that you might ask your assistant to look into:

- *Realty Income Corporation (O):* Often referred to as "The Monthly Dividend Company," Realty Income is renowned for its dependable monthly dividends, primarily derived from its diversified portfolio of over 6,500 real estate properties. This stock is my personal favorite, has made me the most money (in regards to dividends), and is the bulk of my portfolio holdings.

- *STAG Industrial, Inc. (STAG):* This company focuses on industrial real estate and has established a reputation for consistent monthly dividend payments. They are most notable to me as the real estate company that leases buildings and warehouses to Amazon. Yes, Amazon pays them rent.

- *EPR Properties (EPR):* Engaging in properties within the entertainment and education sectors, EPR Properties is another notable company offering monthly dividends.

Taking Action

To invest in monthly dividend stocks, *coordination* with your outside assistant is crucial. They can help you:

- Sign into your brokerage account (remembering the details from our earlier sections on setting one up).

- Research and purchase shares in the identified monthly dividend stocks.
- Track your dividends to ensure they are being paid out as expected.

IN SUMMARY, MONTHLY DIVIDEND STOCKS OFFER A PRACTICAL option for those seeking steady income and the potential benefits of more frequent payouts. By conducting thorough research and utilizing your assistant's help, you can make informed decisions and take advantage of these unique investment opportunities even while incarcerated.

REALTY INCOME: THE MONTHLY DIVIDEND STOCK

OKAY, SO I HAD TO DO THIS. I HAD TO GIVE Y'ALL A MORE thorough breakdown of dividends, REITs, and my favorite company which happens to consist of both, *Realty Income.*

Now, again, I know investing can seem complicated from behind the wall, but you can still take meaningful steps toward financial growth. As stated earlier, one of the fascinating categories in the stock market is dividend stocks — companies that pay a portion of their earnings to shareholders regularly. Among them is a company known as

Realty Income, often referred to as "The Monthly Dividend Company", In this section, we'll break down what makes Realty Income a unique and profitable choice for many investors.

WHAT IS REALTY INCOME?

REALTY INCOME, OFFICIALLY KNOWN AS REALTY INCOME Corporation, is a real estate investment trust (REIT). A *REIT* is a company that owns, operates, or finances income-producing real estate. Realty Income primarily invests in commercial properties such as retail stores, theaters, fitness centers, and more. Some of their most notable tenants are FedEx, Dollar General, Family Dollar, Dollar Tree, Lowe's, Chipotle, 7-Eleven, Walgreens, Sainsbury's (a blue chip grocery operator in the UK), and in 2022, they purchased the Wynn Encore Boston Harbor Resort and Casino for $1.7 billion at a 5.9% cash cap rate. Realty Income is dope!

Listen... and I'm not attempting to sell you on the stock, but I do want you to understand REITs, and in my opinion, yet arguably, the most dominant REIT of our time. Companies like the ones listed above as tenants sell products, gas, entertainment, etc., but they DON'T BUILD PROPERTIES!!

That means they have to go to companies who lease them space, and unlike us who generally sign one-year leases, these companies sign twenty-to-thirty-year leases. Can you imagine FedEx paying you rent? Or Lowe's? How about Chipotle? A lot of these companies have been around since we can remember, some before we were even thought of. Chipotle itself is an industry leader. The likelihood of them all falling off is slim to none.

All in all, its uniqueness lies in its reputability and its unwavering commitment to paying monthly dividends. Since their founding, they have declared 648 consecutive monthly dividends and are a member of the S&P 500 Dividend Aristocrats® index, having increased their dividend for the last thirty consecutive years as of the publishing of this book (2025).

What is a Monthly Dividend?

Most companies pay dividends quarterly (every three months), making the flow of income more sporadic. However, Realty Income distinguishes itself by paying dividends monthly. Think of dividends as little payments you receive just for owning the stock. For incarcerated investors, this could mean a more steady and frequent income, making it ideal for any outside assistant who helps you manage your investments.

. . .

WHY IS REALTY INCOME APPEALING?

1. *Consistency:* Realty Income is famous for reliable and consistent dividend payments. It has paid monthly dividends for over twenty-five years and has increased the dividend every year. This makes it a stable investment choice compared to other stocks that might have fluctuating dividend payments.

2. *Strong Tenant Base:* The company leases its properties to high-quality tenants, typically under long-term contracts, so there is a lower risk of tenants leaving or defaulting. This stability directly translates into reliable income that supports those steady monthly dividends.

3. *Less Volatility:* Stocks in the real estate sector, especially REITs, tend to be less volatile compared to other sectors. This means you're less likely to experience wild swings in the stock price, making it a less stressful investment while you're in prison.

4. *Attractive Yields:* The yield is the amount of cash that returns to you on the investment. Realty Income often provides attractive yields, meaning you get a decent amount of return for what you invest.

. . .

Is Realty Income Recession Proof?

SINCE GOING PUBLIC IN 1994, REALTY INCOME HAS PRODUCED 13.9% annualized returns, handily outperforming the S&P 500. The stock also has a 5.6% dividend yield and has increased the monthly payout for 106 consecutive quarters, even during recessions.

How to Invest in Realty Income from Prison

1. *Educate Your Assistant:* Share the information about Realty Income and its benefits. They should understand why this stock is a good fit for your investment strategy.
2. *Setting Up a Brokerage Account:* Your assistant will need to set up or use an existing brokerage account where they can buy stocks on your behalf. Choose a reputable brokerage with low fees.
3. *Funds Transfer:* Arrange for the transfer of funds into the brokerage account. This might come from

any savings you have or other sources of funds you trust.

4. *Purchase Stocks:* Instruct your assistant to buy shares of Realty Income (stock ticker symbol: O). They can do this online through the brokerage account.

5. *Monitor and Reinvest:* Ensure that your assistant keeps track of the dividends paid out each month. Dividends can be reinvested to buy more shares of Realty Income or into other investment opportunities, further increasing your wealth over time.

BY INVESTING IN REALTY INCOME, YOU ARE SETTING UP A consistent and reliable income stream that can be managed even from behind bars. This strategy can provide a sense of financial security and a foundation for further investment opportunities down the line.

Introduction to Options Trading

"It's not whether you're right or wrong, but how much money you make when you're right and how much you lose when you're wrong."
George Soros

One of the intriguing aspects of the stock market is options trading. In this section, we will explore the basics and help you understand how options can be a part of your investment strategy.

WHAT ARE STOCK OPTIONS?

. . .

TO BREAK IT DOWN SIMPLY, A *STOCK OPTION* IS A CONTRACT that gives you *the right*, but not the obligation, to buy or sell a stock at a specified price within a certain period. Think of it as a way to "lock in" a price for a stock, even if you don't own it yet. This can be highly beneficial if you believe the price of the stock is going to move in a direction that will be profitable for you.

TYPES OF STOCK OPTIONS

THERE ARE TWO MAIN TYPES OF STOCK OPTIONS:

- *Call Options:* These give you the right to buy a stock at a certain price, known as the "strike price", before a specified expiration date. You might buy a call option if you believe the stock price will go up. For example, if you have a call option for a stock at $10 and the stock goes up to $15, you could buy the stock for $10 and potentially make a profit.
- *Put Options:* These give you the right to sell a stock at the strike price before the expiration date. You might buy a put option if you believe the stock price will go down. Using the same example, if you have a put option for a stock at

$10 and the stock falls to $5, you could still sell it for $10.

Key Terms to Know

- To fully grasp stock options, here are some essential terms: *Strike Price:* The price at which you can buy (in case of call options) or sell (in case of put options) the stock.
- *Expiration Date:* The date by which you must exercise your option (either buy or sell the stock), or it will expire.
- *Premium:* The price you pay to buy the option. This is like a fee for the opportunity to buy or sell the stock at the strike price.
- *In-the-Money:* If exercising the option leads to a profit, it is said to be "in-the-money".
- *Out-of-the-Money:* If exercising the option would not lead to a profit, it's known as "out-of-the-money".

Utilizing an Outside Assistant

. . .

- Since you are currently incarcerated, you'll need to rely on an outside assistant to handle the transactions. It's important to clearly communicate the specifics of the options you want to trade, including: The type of option (call or put).
- The strike price.
- The expiration date.
- The amount of premium you are willing to pay.

MAKE SURE YOU TRUST AND HAVE A SOLID UNDERSTANDING with this assistant to avoid any communication mistakes, as options trading can be time-sensitive and require quick actions.

RISKS AND REWARDS

OPTIONS CAN OFFER SIGNIFICANT REWARDS, BUT THEY ALSO come with risks. The premium you pay is non-refundable, meaning if the stock doesn't move as anticipated, you lose the money spent on the option. This is where the most money in the market is gained — and also lost. It's essential to balance the potential for high returns with the risk of loss.

Understanding and utilizing stock options can be a powerful addition to your investment strategy, even from prison. With the assistance of a trusted outside helper, you can take advantage of market movements and potentially achieve financial gains. As always, make sure to conduct thorough research and consider seeking professional advice to make well-informed decisions.

RISKS OF OPTIONS TRADING:

I. **Potential for Complete Loss:**
   - *Time Decay:* One of the significant risks with options is that they have an expiration date. If the expected price movement doesn't occur within the option's life, the option can expire worthless, leading to a complete loss of the premium paid.

   - *Market Volatility:* The value of options can be highly volatile. Rapid fluctuations in the stock price can lead to significant losses, especially if you are trading with leverage.

3. Complexity and Learning Curve:

- *Advanced Knowledge Required:* Options trading can be complex and requires a sound understanding of various strategies, terms, and market behaviors. Mistakes due to a lack of knowledge can be costly.
- *Need for Active Management:* Successful options trading often requires closely monitoring the market and your positions, which can be challenging without direct access. You'll need a reliable outside assistant who can act quickly on your instructions.

4. Brokerage and Commission Costs:

- *Transaction Costs:* Trading options can involve higher commissions and fees compared to regular stock trading. These costs can eat into your profits or exacerbate your losses, so it's essential to factor them into your trading strategy.

．　．　．

MAKING INFORMED DECISIONS IN OPTIONS TRADING IS CRUCIAL. Here are a few tips to manage the risks:

- *Education:* Continually educate yourself about different options strategies and market conditions. Books, online courses, and simulation tools can be beneficial.
- *Start Small:* Begin with simpler strategies and smaller positions. As you gain more experience and confidence, you can proceed to more complex strategies and larger trades.
- *Risk Management:* Always have a risk management plan. Know your risk tolerance and set stop-loss orders to limit potential losses.

REWARDS OF OPTIONS TRADING:

1. High Profit Potential:

- Leverage: Options provide investors with the ability to control large amounts of stock for a relatively small investment. This is due to the leverage options offer. If the stock moves in the direction you anticipated, the percentage gains can be significantly higher compared to directly owning the stock.

- Flexibility: Options trading offers various strategies to make money. Whether the market is going up, down, or sideways, there is likely an options strategy that can be employed to potentially profit from the situation.

- Defined Risk: When buying options, your maximum loss is typically limited to the amount you paid for the option. This can help manage and define your risk, which is critical for those looking to avoid unexpected large losses.

  1. Income Generation:

- Selling Options: Investors can generate income by selling options. For instance, selling covered calls against stocks you already own can provide additional income. This can be an excellent strategy for generating cash flow.

  1. Risk Management and Hedging:

- Protection for Your Portfolio: Options can be used to hedge against potential losses in your portfolio. By purchasing put options, you can secure a sell price for your stocks, ensuring you limit losses if the market takes a downturn.

. . .

OPTIONS TRADING OFFERS BOTH EXCITING OPPORTUNITIES AND considerable risks. By understanding these risks and rewards and working closely with a trusted outside assistant, you can make informed and strategic decisions in your investment journey. Remember, every great investor started with a small step, and with careful learning and planning, you can turn even the smallest opportunities into significant gains.

Risk Management Strategies for Inmates

"Understanding risks is the first step to mastering your investment journey."
Chris Sain

<u>Importance of Risk Management</u>

First, I have to start this chapter off by saying this: DON'T GO OUT BAD!! Investing in the stock market is similar to participating in a high-stakes game: it holds the potential for significant rewards, but also comes with an inherent set of risks. For incarcerated individuals, managing this risk effectively is not just a good strategy — it's *an essential* one. Understanding the importance of risk management can be the difference between potentially doubling your investment and losing your hard-earned capital. Let's break it down.

1. **Protecting Your Capital:**
   - *Definition: Capital* refers to the initial money you invest in the stock market. For most, this capital is hard-earned, whether through prison jobs, savings, or support from friends and family.

   - *Significance:* Protecting this capital should be your primary goal. If you lose your capital, you can't continue to invest or grow your wealth. Risk management strategies, such as diversifying your investments (spreading your money across various stocks or other assets), help in safeguarding your principal amount.

3. **Reducing Anxiety and Uncertainty:**
   - *Definition:* Investing can be an emotional rollercoaster, especially when you see your money fluctuating on a daily basis.

- ○ *Significance:* Proper risk management can provide a sense of control and reduce stress. It involves setting stop-loss orders (instructions to sell a stock when it reaches a certain price) and determining the maximum amount you're willing to lose on a single investment. These measures ensure that you are prepared for the worst-case scenarios and can make clear-headed decisions.

4. **Maximizing Long-term Gains:**
   - ○ *Definition:* While it's tempting to go for high-risk, high-reward stocks, these are often not sustainable long-term strategies for most investors.
   - ○ *Significance:* Effective risk management involves balancing your portfolio with a mix of high-risk and low-risk investments. This strategy increases the chances of steady, long-term growth rather than short-term gains followed by heart-breaking losses. For instance, investing in well-established, blue-chip stocks might offer smaller returns but are generally less volatile compared to speculative stocks.

5. Learning and Growth:
    - *Definition:* Managing risk is not just about avoiding losses; it's also about understanding the market and improving your investment skills.

- *Significance:* By analytically assessing the risks and making informed decisions, you'll gradually become a more knowledgeable investor. This experience is invaluable, especially when your access to real-time information and trading platforms is limited. For example, regularly reviewing your portfolio or performance reports with the help of your outside assistant can offer insights into what strategies are working and which ones aren't.

5. **Building Trust with Your Assistant:**
    - *Definition:* Since you will need an outside assistant to execute most of your trades and manage logistics, it's paramount to have a trusting and transparent relationship.

○ *Significance:* By adopting sound risk management practices, you can clearly communicate your investment strategies and risk tolerance to your assistant. This mutual understanding can prevent misunderstandings and mistakes. For instance, ensure that your assistant knows your risk thresholds and the importance of diversifying your investment portfolio.

IN SUMMARY, UNDERSTANDING THE IMPORTANCE OF RISK management and implementing it effectively can set the foundation for not just surviving but thriving in your stock market ventures. By protecting your capital, reducing anxiety, maximizing long-term gains, fostering learning, and building trust with your assistant, you create a well-rounded approach to tackling the stock market from within prison walls. This disciplined approach will enable you to navigate the ups and downs of the market with confidence and clarity.

SETTING STOP-LOSS ORDERS

. . .

ONE OF THE MOST IMPORTANT ASPECTS OF INVESTING IN THE stock market is *managing your risk.* Since you're in a unique situation where you cannot constantly monitor your investments, implementing risk management strategies like setting stop-loss orders can protect your portfolio from significant losses. Let's break down what stop-loss orders are and how you can effectively use them with the help of your outside assistant.

What is a Stop-Loss Order?

A *STOP-LOSS ORDER* IS A PRE-SET INSTRUCTION TO SELL A particular stock when its price falls to a certain level. The primary purpose of a stop-loss order is to limit your loss on a stock that might be declining. Think of it as a safety net that automatically gets activated to prevent you from losing more money than you are comfortable with.

For example, if you purchased a share at $100, you might place a stop-loss order at $90. If the stock price drops to $90, your outside assistant — following your instructions — will automatically sell the stock. This way, you limit your loss to $10 per share.

Why are Stop-Loss Orders Important?

. . .

1. *Minimized Losses:* Without a stop-loss order, you could potentially lose a lot more if the stock price keeps going down. This automated strategy ensures you exit a failing investment before losses deepen.

2. *Peace of Mind:* Being incarcerated makes it challenging to keep a daily watch on the stock market. Stop-loss orders help in mitigating the risk by providing a level of automatization.

3. *Discipline:* Emotions can sometimes cloud judgment in investing. Setting predetermined levels for stop-losses helps to stick to your risk management plan without letting fear or greed dictate your actions.

SETTING STOP-LOSS ORDERS WITH AN ASSISTANT

NOW, THIS IS SOME GAME I WISH I WOULD'VE HAD BEFORE I tried my hand at trading. An options play that I made at the start of the year, January 2024, in the company 1-800-FLOWERS (FLWS) cost me nearly a $3,500 loss. Earnings was approaching for the company, and I had played a call, predicting the company to go up. In my mind, it *had* to. After all, Valentine's Day was next month. There was no way they would fail to meet earnings. Was I right? Kind of. They did beat earnings... but the stock still plummeted. That happened with a lot of companies in 2024. I had no stop-loss, and everything that I put in was gone.

That's why it is crucial to choose someone you trust to handle these tasks on your behalf. Here's how you can set a stop-loss order:

1. *Identify Your Comfort Level:* Decide how much loss you are willing to tolerate. This will vary depending on your risk appetite and investment strategy.
2. *Communicate Clearly:* Make sure your outside assistant understands your instructions clearly. Specify at what price the stop-loss should be set.
3. *Utilize Technology:* Today, many brokerage platforms allow setting stop-loss orders online. Your assistant can do this via a brokerage account that you have set up.
4. *Regular Updates:* Ask for regular updates on your investments. Your assistant can update you on the performance and make necessary adjustments to stop-loss orders as required.

CALCULATING THE STOP-LOSS LEVEL

HERE'S A SIMPLE STRATEGY TO CALCULATE WHERE TO PLACE your stop-loss order:

1. *Determine Your Entry Point:* Identify the price point at which you bought the stock.
2. *Define Your Loss Limit:* Decide the maximum percentage of loss you're comfortable with. A common range is between five percent and twenty percent, depending on the stock's volatility and your risk tolerance.
3. *Calculate the Stop-Loss Price:* Subtract the loss limit (in dollar terms) from your entry point. For example, if you purchased a stock at $50 and set a loss limit at ten percent, your stop-loss price would be $45.

EXAMPLE:

Let's say you purchased shares of XYZ Company at $100 each. You've decided that you don't want to lose more than ten percent on that investment. Here's how you would set up your stop-loss order:

1. L-Entry Price: $100
2. Loss Limit: 10%
3. Stop-Loss Price: 100 – (100 x 0.10) = $90

You then instruct your assistant to place a stop-loss order at $90. If the share price drops to this level, the stop-loss order will automatically execute, and the shares will be sold.

In summary, setting stop-loss orders is a crucial part of managing risk in the stock market, especially when you cannot actively monitor your investments. By clearly communicating your stop-loss levels to a trusted outside assistant, you can protect your investment portfolio and have greater peace of mind.

Limiting Exposure to Risky Investments

When you're new to investing, it's important to understand that not all investments are created equal. Some have higher risks attached to them, meaning there's a greater chance that their value could drop suddenly and drastically. As an inmate, it's crucial to protect your hard-earned money by limiting your exposure to these risky investments. Let's break down what this means and how you can go about it.

Understanding Risky Investments

Risky investments are those where the potential for high rewards comes with the possibility of significant losses. Some examples include:

- *Penny Stocks:* These are stocks of very small companies. They usually trade for less than $5 per share and can be incredibly volatile.
- *Cryptocurrencies:* Digital currencies like Bitcoin can have wild price swings. While some have made fortunes, others have lost significant sums almost overnight.
- *Options and Futures:* These are financial instruments that can amplify your gains but also your losses. They require a deep understanding to manage effectively.

They do have Discords and trading communities that will give you the plays, then all you have to do is handle the business. But everyone is not to be trusted and please avoid scammers. Tell your people not to click on random links, because they can be hack link traps. Also, not everyone with a YouTube or Instagram that posts about stocks is a trading expert. The most affordable and accurate options trader to get weekly plays from that I've come across is Chris Sain. Go to his website and join The Money Team. Costs you $250 a week, and it doesn't have to be an every week thing. Whenever you want some plays that can make you thousands, spend that little 250. Also, for the same amount, you can talk with him on the phone and get a full rundown of the market and how to build a winning portfolio.

Is it worth it? I think so. I've done it only a couple times, and it was always money well spent. I haven't got on the phone with him yet, but I do plan to in the near future. In Chapter 13, I speak more about him and other notable African American investors. TAP IN!!

WHY LIMIT EXPOSURE?

1. *Volatility:* Risky investments can fluctuate widely in value, making them unpredictable.
2. *Losses:* High-risk investments can wipe out a large portion of your initial capital.

3. *Stress and Uncertainty:* Watching the value of your investments swing wildly can cause unnecessary stress, which is particularly unhelpful in a prison setting.

PRACTICAL STEPS FOR LIMITING EXPOSURE

SINCE YOU'LL NEED OUTSIDE ASSISTANCE TO MANAGE YOUR investments, communicate clearly with your assistant about your risk tolerance and strategy. Here's how to limit your exposure:

1. *Diversify Your Portfolio:* Don't put all your eggs in one basket. Spread your investments across different types of assets like stocks, bonds, and mutual funds. This way, if one investment performs poorly, others might still do well, balancing your overall portfolio.

2. *Invest in Blue-Chip Stocks:* These are shares in large, well-established, and financially sound companies. They are considered safer and more reliable over the long term.

3. *Consider Index Funds:* These funds track a specific market index like the S&P 500. They offer broad

market exposure and tend to be less volatile than individual stocks.

4. *Set a Risk Limit:* Decide on a percentage of your total investment portfolio that can be allocated to high-risk investments. For example, you might limit risky investments to no more than ten percent of your total funds.

5. *Regular Check-Ins:* Schedule regular check-ins with your assistant to review your portfolio's performance and make adjustments as needed. This ensures that your investments are aligned with your risk tolerance and financial goals.

6. *Educate Yourself Continuously:* Even though you rely on an assistant, the more you understand about investing, the better you can guide their actions. Read books, take correspondence courses, and stay informed about financial news.

USING STOP-LOSS ORDERS

A STOP-LOSS ORDER CAN BE A USEFUL TOOL TO PROTECT YOUR investments. It automatically sells a security when it reaches a certain price, reducing the emotional burden of deciding when to cut losses. Ensure your assistant understands how to implement stop-loss orders for particularly risky investments. Have them go to YouTube and search "How To Set A Stop Loss On Options In Robinhood," or whatever brokerage you're using. If it's TD Ameritrade search, "How To Set A Stop Loss On Options In TD Ameritrade." Whatever they need to know how to do, trust me... it's on YouTube. Some things your outside assistant may need to learn, and that doesn't mean they will always get it right. Be patient with them. You are both first generation wealth builders. This is foreign territory. But the more we learn, the better we get, and the better we get, the more profitable our returns are. You're the coach. Build your team and call the plays.

CONCLUSION

By understanding what constitutes a risky investment and taking deliberate steps to limit your exposure, you're employing a smart risk management strategy. This approach helps safeguard your capital and sets a strong foundation for long-term investments. Remember, prudent investing is not just about making money — it's also about preserving it.

Building a Long-Term Investment Portfolio

"Educate yourself on financial principles, start investing early, and maintain
a long-term vision to capitalize on the power of compounding."

Mellody Hobson
(Co-CEO and President of Ariel Investments)

<u>Setting Up a Diversified Stock Portfolio</u>

A KEY PRINCIPLE IN INVESTING IS *DIVERSIFICATION*. IN SIMPLE terms, diversification is like not putting all your eggs in one basket. If one basket falls and breaks, you'll still have eggs in another one. In the context of the stock market, this means not putting all your money into one company or one sector.

Instead, you spread your investments across various types of stocks to reduce the risk of losing your money. When done correctly, diversification helps you weather the ups and downs of the stock market by balancing out losses with gains elsewhere.

In this chapter, you'll learn how to set up a well-rounded stock portfolio while working with the limitations of your situation. While access to technology is restricted for you, that will not prevent you from building a long-term investment portfolio with guidance and support from your trusted outside contact. Let's dive into the steps to achieve this.

STEP 1: EDUCATE YOURSELF ON STOCKS

Before you can start building your portfolio, you need to understand the basics of stocks. A stock represents a share of ownership in a company. When you buy a stock, you're essentially buying a small piece of that company. Stock prices go up and down based on how well the company is doing and general market conditions.

THERE ARE PRIMARILY TWO TYPES OF STOCKS YOU SHOULD BE aware of:

1. Common Stocks: These are the most basic form of stock ownership. They typically give shareholders voting

rights and may pay dividends (a share of the company's profits).

2. Preferred Stocks: These don't usually come with voting rights, but they tend to have higher and consistent dividends. For this chapter, we'll focus on common stocks, as they provide more opportunities for growth over time.

USE BOOKS, NEWSLETTERS, OR OTHER OUTSIDE PRINTED sources to deepen your understanding of the stock market. Make note of stock market terms and concepts you come across, as this will help you make better decisions and direct your outside contact more effectively.

STEP 2: DETERMINE YOUR INVESTMENT BUDGET

Your starting budget will determine how much money you can invest, but it's important to emphasize that investing is not a one-time decision — it's an ongoing process. Even with a small amount to begin with, you can build a substantial portfolio over time through consistent investing.

If you're starting with limited funds, you might instruct your outside contact to look into brokers that allow *fractional shares* — this means buying a small piece of a stock rather than having to purchase a full share. Fractional shares allow you to invest in expensive companies like Apple or Amazon without needing thousands of dollars upfront.

. . .

Step 3: Learn About Diversification in the Stock Market

Building a diversified portfolio of stocks means spreading your investments across:

1. Different Industries: For example, instead of investing all your money in technology companies, you could spread it across technology, healthcare, consumer goods, and utilities. This way, if one sector experiences a downturn, your investments in other sectors may stay strong or even grow.

2. Company Sizes (Market Capitalization): Stocks can be categorized as large-cap, mid-cap, or small-cap. By investing in a mix of these, you can balance between stability (large-cap stocks) and growth potential (small-cap stocks).

- Large-cap: Established companies with a market cap over $10 billion (e.g., Coca-Cola, Amazon).

- Mid-cap: Companies with a market cap between $2 billion and $10 billion that are in a IPO Growth phase.

- Small-cap: Emerging companies or startups with a market cap under $2 billion that have higher growth potential but also higher risk.

3. Growth vs. Value Stocks:

- Growth stocks: These are companies that are expected to grow faster than their industry average (e.g., tech startups or innovative firms). They often reinvest profits into the business, so they may not pay dividends.

- Value stocks: These are companies that are undervalued by the market but are fundamentally strong. They often pay dividends, which is a steady stream of passive income.

4. REIT Stocks (Real Estate Investment Trusts): While you can't invest in physical real estate, you can diversify into real estate through REIT stocks. REITs are companies that own or finance income-producing real estate, like office buildings or shopping malls. These can provide consistent dividends and growth over time.

STEP 4: PRIORITIZE LONG-TERM INVESTMENT STRATEGIES

The stock market rewards patience. While short-term trading might sound exciting, it carries higher risks and requires constant monitoring—something outside of your practical capabilities. Instead, it's better to focus on buy-and-hold investing.

BUY-AND-HOLD INVESTING MEANS PURCHASING STOCKS OF good companies and holding onto them for years, even decades. Over time, the stock market historically trends upward, and long-term investors are able to ride out the market's short-term fluctuations.

. . .

EMPHASIZE TO YOUR OUTSIDE CONTACT THAT THE GOAL IS TO buy quality, reliable stocks with strong growth potential or consistent dividends. Look for companies with a track record of good financial health, solid leadership, and a strong market position.

STEP 5: HOW TO DIRECT YOUR OUTSIDE CONTACT

SINCE YOU WON'T BE DIRECTLY ACCESSING THE STOCK MARKET, it's crucial to provide clear instructions to your trusted outside contact who will handle transactions on your behalf. Follow these guidelines:

1. Research Specific Companies: Instruct your contact to look into companies you've identified or ones you're interested in. Use your knowledge to guide their research—this will help them act in your best interest.

EXAMPLE: YOU COULD SAY, "LOOK UP COMPANIES LIKE Microsoft, Walmart, and Visa. Let me know their recent stock prices and news about their earnings or growth."

. . .

2. Evaluate Stock Prices: Encourage your contact to compare current stock prices with the companies' earnings performance and growth projections. Stocks that are overpriced may not be the best choice, even if they're popular.

3. Keep Transaction Costs Low: Instruct your contact to find a brokerage firm that has low or no trading fees. Excessive fees can eat into your profits over time.

4. Create a Consistent Investment Schedule: Advise your contact to put money into the market regularly, even if it's a small amount. This strategy, called dollar-cost averaging, means buying stocks at different price levels over time. This reduces the risk of investing all your money when prices are high.

STEP 6: TRACK AND REASSESS YOUR PORTFOLIO

ALTHOUGH YOU'LL BE HOLDING YOUR INVESTMENTS FOR THE long term, that doesn't mean you should "set it and forget it." Provide your outside contact with regular instructions to check in on your portfolio's performance and make adjustments if needed.

FOR EXAMPLE:

1. IF ONE SECTOR OF THE MARKET HAS GROWN TOO MUCH, YOUR portfolio may become unbalanced. You can ask your contact to "rebalance" by selling some shares in that sector and reinvesting the profits in an underrepresented area.

2. If a company starts to show signs of deterioration—like leadership scandals, declining profits, or increasing debt—it may be time to sell your shares in that company and reinvest elsewhere.

STEP 7: PATIENCE IS THE KEY TO SUCCESS

. . .

IN THE STOCK MARKET, WEALTH IS OFTEN BUILT OVER TIME, NOT overnight. You might encounter ups and downs, but remember that temporary market declines are part of the process. Stay focused on your long-term goals, and don't get discouraged by short-term setbacks.

INVESTMENT IS POWER

INVESTING IN STOCKS FROM PRISON MAY SOUND CHALLENGING, but it is entirely possible with discipline, knowledge, and the help of a reliable outside contact. By educating yourself on stock market principles, spreading your investments appropriately, and maintaining a consistent, long-term approach, you can build wealth for your future.

THE STOCK MARKET HAS CREATED WEALTH FOR COUNTLESS people, and it can do the same for you. Even in your current circumstances, you have the tools to take control of your financial future.

UNDERSTANDING DIVERSIFICATION

. . .

Diversification is like not putting all your eggs in one basket. If one basket falls, you still have some eggs in other baskets. In investing, this means not putting all your money into one type of asset or one single company. Instead, you spread your investment across different types of financial instruments, industries, and other categories to minimize risk.

Types of Assets

To diversify, you should consider investing in various types of assets. Here are some common types:

1. *Stocks:* Shares of individual companies. Stocks can be further diversified by investing in companies from different sectors (e.g., technology, healthcare, energy).

2. *Bonds:* Loans you give to companies or governments that pay you interest. Bonds are generally considered less risky than stocks.

. . .

3. *Mutual Funds:* Pooled funds from many investors to buy a diversified portfolio of stocks, bonds, or other assets.

4. *ETFs (Exchange-Traded Funds):* Like mutual funds but traded on the stock exchange. They offer an easy way to diversify.

5. *Real Estate:* Property investments, which can offer income and increase in value over time. (Note: Real estate might be more challenging to manage without assistance, but Real Estate Investment Trusts (REITs) like Realty Income are an alternative to consider.)

ALLOCATING YOUR PORTFOLIO

. . .

HOW YOU ALLOCATE YOUR INVESTMENTS ACROSS THESE ASSET types depends on your risk tolerance and investment horizon (how long you plan to invest). Here are some examples:

- *Conservative Portfolio:* For lower risk, you might allocate more to bonds and less to stocks. For example, 70% bonds, 20% stocks, and 10% in other assets like real estate or commodities.

- *Balanced Portfolio:* A mix of risk and stability. For example, 50% stocks, 40% bonds, and 10% in other assets.

- *Aggressive Portfolio:* Higher risk with potential for higher returns. For example, 80% stocks, 15% bonds, and 5% in other assets.

PRACTICAL STEPS TO START DIVERSIFYING

1. *Research:* Investigate the different types of assets. Look at historical performance, risk factors, and how they might fit into your overall goals.

2. *Set Up Accounts:* Your assistant can help you open brokerage or investment accounts needed to buy the diversified assets.

3. *Start Small:* Begin with small investments to minimize initial risk. Gradually increase your investments as you become more comfortable and knowledgeable.

4. *Monitor and Rebalance:* Regularly check how your investments are performing. You or your assistant might need to rebalance – adjust the mix of assets to maintain the desired level of diversification.

By setting up a diversified portfolio, you can reduce risk while working toward your long-term investment goals. It might seem complex at first but breaking it down into these steps makes it manageable, even from prison. Your financial future is something you can start building today, even from behind bars.

Rebalancing Investments Periodically

Rebalancing your investments is a critical strategy in maintaining a healthy long-term investment portfolio. It's like maintaining a car: regular check-ups and fixes are necessary to keep it running smoothly. In the context of your investments, rebalancing means adjusting the amounts you have invested in different types of assets, such as stocks, bonds, and cash to maintain your desired balance and to manage risk effectively.

Here's how it works and why it's important:

1. **Understanding Asset Allocation:**

ASSET ALLOCATION IS THE PROCESS OF DIVIDING YOUR investments among different categories or asset classes, like stocks, bonds, and cash. The goal is to balance risk and reward according to your personal risk tolerance and investment time frame. For example, a common allocation might be 60% stocks, 30% bonds, and 10% cash.

2. Changes in the Market:

OVER TIME, THE MARKET VALUES OF THESE ASSETS WILL change. Stocks might go up in value, while bonds could go down, or vice versa. These changes can distort your initial asset allocation. For example, if your stocks have performed very well, your portfolio might shift to 70% stocks, 20% bonds, and 10% cash. This new allocation could expose you to more risk than you initially intended because you now have a higher percentage in stocks, which are generally riskier than bonds.

3. Rebalancing to Original Allocation:

To correct this, you would sell some of the assets that have increased in value (in this case, stocks) and buy more of the assets that have decreased in value (bonds or cash) to get back to your original allocation of 60% stocks, 30% bonds, and 10% cash. This process is known as *rebalancing*. It ensures that you stay disciplined and don't let the market's movements determine your risk exposure.

4. Frequency of Rebalancing:

There isn't a one-size-fits-all answer to how often you should rebalance. However, a common practice is to do it periodically. This could be once a year, semi-annually, or even quarterly, depending on your preference and the specifics of your investment plan. There's also a method where you rebalance only when your allocation deviates by a certain percentage from your target.

5. Involving Your Outside Assistants:

SINCE YOU'RE INVESTING FROM PRISON, YOU'LL NEED THE HELP of your outside assistant to monitor your portfolio's performance and to execute the rebalancing transactions. It's essential to communicate your rebalancing strategy clearly to them. Provide detailed instructions on when and how to rebalance based on the parameters you've set. You might set up regular check-ins with your assistant to review your portfolio and ensure that rebalancing happens as planned.

6. Benefits of Rebalancing:

THE PRIMARY ADVANTAGE OF REBALANCING IS MAINTAINING your desired level of risk. It helps you avoid becoming too heavily invested in any one asset class and ensures that you're taking advantage of the principles of "buy low, sell high." By selling assets that have increased in value and buying those that have declined, you're systematically buying low and selling high.

7. Challenges and Costs:

While rebalancing is crucial, it's not without its challenges. There can be transaction costs associated with buying and selling assets, and in taxable accounts, selling assets at a gain could incur capital gains taxes. It's important to weigh these costs against the benefits of maintaining your desired asset allocation. Discuss potential costs with your assistant and consider ways to minimize them, such as using tax-advantaged accounts like IRAs if possible.

By understanding and implementing a rebalancing strategy, you'll be well on your way to maintaining a disciplined, long-term investment portfolio. This steady approach can help protect your investments from the volatility of the market and keep you on track towards achieving your financial goals, even while managing from a distance.

Monitoring and Adjusting Your Portfolio as Needed

Once you've created a solid investment portfolio, it's crucial to monitor and adjust it regularly to ensure it continues to meet your financial goals. Even though you may be physically restricted, you can still manage this aspect effectively with the help of an outside assistant and a defined strategy. Here's how you can stay on top of your investments and make needed adjustments:

1. REGULAR PORTFOLIO REVIEWS

YOUR INVESTMENT ASSISTANT SHOULD CONDUCT REGULAR reviews of your portfolio. This can be monthly, quarterly, or at any other interval that suits your investment strategy. The main purpose of these reviews is to:

- *Assess Performance:* Evaluate how well your investments are performing. Look at key indicators such as gains, losses, and overall growth.

- *Check Alignment with Goals:* Ensure that your portfolio still aligns with your long-term financial goals. Circumstances can change, and your investment strategy might need tweaks to stay on track.

2. Rebalancing Your Portfolio

Over time, some investments in your portfolio might grow faster than others, leading to an imbalance. For example, if tech stocks perform exceptionally well, they might take up a larger portion of your portfolio than you originally intended. *Rebalancing* is the process of adjusting your investments back to your target asset allocation.

- *Identify Imbalances:* Have your assistant track the percentage of each asset class in your portfolio and compare them to your target allocations.
- *Make Adjustments:* To rebalance, you might sell some of the over-performing assets and reinvest in the under-performing ones. This can help manage risk and maintain diversification.

3. Staying Informed

Though your access to information is limited, staying informed about market trends and economic changes is crucial. Your assistant can help by:

. . .

- *Providing Updates:* Regularly bring you news and reports on market conditions and how they may affect your investments.
- *Interpreting Data:* Simplify complex financial information so you can make informed decisions without getting overwhelmed.

4. EVALUATING INVESTMENT CHOICES

MARKETS FLUCTUATE AND NEW INVESTMENT OPPORTUNITIES arise. Periodically evaluate the individual investments in your portfolio:

- *Performance Metrics:* Check key metrics like earnings growth, profit margins, and stock performance relative to peers.
- *Business Fundamentals:* Look at changes in the business model, management, and competitive landscape of the companies you're invested in.

5. Adapting to Life Changes

Your personal situation can change, impacting your financial goals and risk tolerance. For instance:

- *Health Changes:* Unexpected medical expenses might require a different financial approach.
- *Legal Changes:* Parole or release could open up new investment possibilities, requiring portfolio adjustment.

6. Communication with Your Assistant

Maintain clear and consistent communication with your assistant. Use phone calls, letters, or any other approved method to:

- *Discuss Strategies:* Review current strategies and potential adjustments.
- *Set Clear Instructions:* Make sure your assistant

understands your long-term goals and the reasons behind any changes.

7. UTILIZING TRUSTED ADVISORS

IF YOUR ASSISTANT ISN'T A FINANCIAL EXPERT, CONSIDER USING trusted financial advisors or services through them:

- *Research Professionals:* Certified Financial Planners (CFPs) or investment advisors can provide expert guidance.
- *Diversified Opinions:* Having multiple perspectives can help in making well-rounded decisions.

CONCLUSION

Monitoring and adjusting your portfolio is a dynamic process that ensures your investments align with your financial goals. By partnering effectively with your assistant and leveraging available resources, you can manage a successful investment portfolio, even from within the confines of prison. Regular reviews, rebalancing, staying informed, and adapting to changes will help you stay on the right track toward achieving your long-term financial aspirations.

Resources for Continued Learning

"The stock market is not a sprint but a marathon. Success comes to those who are patient, willing to learn continuously, and adapt to new information and trends."
Ian Dunlap a.k.a The Master Investor

Recommended Books and Websites for Stock Market Education

TO BUILD A STRONG FOUNDATION IN STOCK MARKET INVESTING, it's crucial to consume a combination of comprehensive textbooks and reputable online resources. For incarcerated individuals, accessibility might be a challenge, but with the help of a supportive friend, family member, or librarian, many of these resources can be obtained. Here's a breakdown of essential books and websites to consider for furthering your stock market education:

BOOKS

1. THE INTELLIGENT INVESTOR BY BENJAMIN GRAHAM

- *Why:* Widely regarded as the bible of investing, this book introduces the concept of value investing and the importance of thorough analysis.
- *Key Topics:* Investment strategies, stock valuation, risk management.

2. ONE UP ON WALL STREET BY PETER LYNCH

- *Why:* Offers sound advice on how to use your existing knowledge to foresee investment opportunities others might overlook.
- *Key Topics:* Spotting growth stocks, long-term investing, practical tips.

3. *A Random Walk Down Wall Street* by Burton G. Malkiel

- *Why:* Provides a comprehensive overview of investment theories and debunks many myths surrounding the stock market.
- *Key Topics:* Efficient Market Hypothesis, various investment strategies, asset allocation.

4. *Common Stocks and Uncommon Profits* by Philip Fisher

- *Why:* Details qualitative aspects of investment research, such as the management's quality and the company's growth potential.
- *Key Topics:* Long-term investing, company analysis, investment philosophy.

Websites

While direct internet access might not be possible in prison, having a loved one or assistant on the outside can help by printing relevant, up-to-date articles and research. Here are a few key websites:

1. INVESTOPEDIA

- *Website:* [www.investopedia.com](https://www. investopedia.comhttps://www.investopedia.com)
- *Why:* Offers a vast library of articles, tutorials, and videos that cover basic and advanced investing concepts in an easy-to-understand manner.
- *Key Features:* Investment guides, stock market news, definitions of financial terms.

2. YAHOO FINANCE

- *Website:* [finance.yahoo.com](https://finance. yahoo.com)
- *Why:* Provides real-time data on stocks, historical price charts, financial statements, and news updates which can be invaluable for market research.
- *Key Features:* Stock screening tools, market trends, expert analysis.

. . .

3. MORNINGSTAR

- *Website:* www.morningstar.com
- *Why:* Known for its in-depth analysis of stocks, mutual funds, and ETFs, it's a great source of unbiased investment research.
- *Key Features:* Analyst reports, investment research, portfolio management tools.

4. THE MOTLEY FOOL

- *Website:* www.fool.com
- *Why:* Offers a mix of free and premium content, including market news, stock analysis, and investment recommendations that are easy to digest.
- *Key Features:* Daily articles, investing podcasts, educational resources.

UTILIZING THESE RESOURCES

. . .

- *Books:* Request these books through your institution's library system. If unavailable, ask a family member or friend to purchase and send them to you.
- *Websites:* Instruct your outside assistant to regularly visit these sites and print out relevant articles, data sheets, and analysis reports to send to you.

By integrating the knowledge from these books and websites into your learning regimen, you'll be well-equipped to make informed investment decisions. Remember, education is an ongoing process, and the more you learn, the more confident and competent you will become in navigating the stock market.

Joining Investment Clubs and Forums Through Correspondence

One of the most effective ways to deepen your understanding of the stock market is to connect with others who share your interest. For incarcerated individuals, joining investment clubs and forums via correspondence can provide a vital lifeline to the broader investing community and ongoing education.

What are Investment Clubs?

INVESTMENT CLUBS ARE GROUPS OF INDIVIDUALS WHO COME together to pool their money and invest in stocks, shares, or other securities. These clubs often function as small-scale investment partnerships where members learn about investing by sharing insights, discussing market trends, and analyzing stocks together. For those who are incarcerated, joining an investment club can be particularly valuable as it offers a structured way to practice and discuss investing strategies.

Why Correspondence?

GIVEN THE LIMITED ACCESS TO THE INTERNET AND OTHER digital resources, correspondence through mail is a feasible and effective way to participate in investment clubs and forums. By writing letters, you can exchange ideas, ask questions, and receive mentorship from experienced investors.

Steps to Joining Investment Clubs and Forums via Correspondence

1. Identify Potential Clubs and Forums

Start by identifying investment clubs and forums that accept correspondence members. Some established clubs and online forums may have programs specifically designed to include incarcerated individuals. You can gather this information through family or friends or through organizations dedicated to prison education and rehabilitation.

2. Seek Assistance from an Outside Partner

Since finding and joining these clubs requires external research, you will need the help of an outside assistant, such as a family member, friend, or volunteer. Provide them with details about your interest and ask them to locate reputable investment clubs and forums where you can participate via mail.

3. WRITE A FORMAL INTRODUCTION

ONCE YOU'VE IDENTIFIED POTENTIAL CLUBS, COMPOSE A formal letter introducing yourself, explaining your situation, and expressing your interest in joining their community. Be sure to highlight your eagerness to learn and your commitment to contributing positively.

SAMPLE INTRODUCTION LETTER:

[YOUR NAME]
    [Inmate ID]
    [Institution Name]
    [Institution Address]
    [Date]

[CLUB/FORUM NAME]
    [Contact Person (if known)]

[Club/Forum Address]

DEAR [CONTACT PERSON/CLUB MEMBERS],

MY NAME IS [YOUR NAME], AND I AM CURRENTLY AN INMATE AT [Institution Name]. I am writing to express my keen interest in joining your investment club/forum through correspondence.

THOUGH I AM INCARCERATED, I AM DEEPLY COMMITTED TO learning about investing in the stock market. I believe that participating in your group would provide me with invaluable knowledge and insights, and I am eager to contribute meaningfully to discussions and activities.

THANK YOU FOR CONSIDERING MY APPLICATION. I LOOK forward to the possibility of enriching my understanding of the stock market with the support of your community.

SINCERELY,
[Your Name]

4. ENGAGE ACTIVELY AND RESPONSIBLY

ONCE YOU HAVE ESTABLISHED CONTACT AND BEEN ACCEPTED into a club or forum, make the most out of the opportunity by actively engaging. Ask questions, share your analyses, and respond thoughtfully to the feedback you receive. Regular correspondence will foster a sense of camaraderie and continuous learning.

5. MAINTAIN RESPECTFUL COMMUNICATION

ALWAYS MAINTAIN RESPECTFUL AND PROFESSIONAL communication. Remember that these clubs and forums are comprised of individuals with diverse backgrounds and expertise. Be open to differing opinions and constructive criticism as it is crucial for your growth as an investor.

BENEFITS OF JOINING INVESTMENT CLUBS AND FORUMS

- *Continuous Learning:* These platforms provide ongoing education about market trends, investment strategies, and financial news.
- *Networking:* Building relationships with experienced investors can lead to mentorship and support.
- *Practical Experience:* Engaging in discussions and analyses helps you practice and refine your investment skills.
- *Community Support:* Being part of a community fosters motivation and accountability, essential for staying committed to your financial education journey.

By participating in investment clubs and forums through correspondence, you can bridge the gap between incarceration and the dynamic world of stock market investing, ensuring that you are continually learning and improving. With dedication and active engagement, these resources can dramatically enhance your investment acumen and prepare you for financial success upon your release.

Seeking Guidance from Financial Advisors Through Trusted Contacts

. . .

NAVIGATING THE INTRICATE WORLD OF THE STOCK MARKET CAN be daunting, especially from within the confines of a prison cell. However, having access to professional guidance can make a significant difference in your investment journey. This is where financial advisors come into play. These professionals are equipped with the knowledge and expertise to help you make informed decisions. Since direct contact with financial advisors may not always be possible from prison, you can leverage the power of your trusted contacts to seek their guidance.

1. Identifying a Reliable Financial Advisor:

START BY ASKING YOUR TRUSTED CONTACTS—FRIENDS, FAMILY members, or your legal advisor—to help you identify a reliable financial advisor. Look for advisors with credible backgrounds, relevant certifications, and positive client reviews. Your contacts can conduct the necessary research on the internet or ask for recommendations from people within their network.

2. Establishing a Communication Channel:

ONCE A SUITABLE ADVISOR IS IDENTIFIED, YOUR TRUSTED contact can establish initial communication. This typically involves explaining your situation, your interest in investing, and the constraints of being incarcerated. The financial advisor needs to understand that most interactions will be indirect, facilitated through your trusted contact.

3. Conveying Your Goals and Constraints:

IT'S ESSENTIAL THAT YOUR TRUSTED CONTACT CONVEYS YOUR financial goals and any constraints you may face, such as limited access to real-time market data or the inability to execute trades directly. The financial advisor can then tailor their advice to fit your unique circumstances. Make sure to communicate your risk tolerance—whether you prefer safe, low-risk investments or are willing to take on higher risks for potentially greater rewards.

4. Regular Updates and Reports:

. . .

YOUR TRUSTED CONTACT CAN ARRANGE FOR REGULAR UPDATES and reports from the financial advisor. These updates can include market analysis, stock recommendations, and performance reviews of your existing investments. You can then review these reports during visits or communication periods with your trusted contact. This way, you stay informed about your portfolio's performance and make necessary adjustments based on the advisor's recommendations.

5. Educational Resources:

FINANCIAL ADVISORS CAN ALSO PROVIDE VALUABLE educational resources like market analyses, newsletters, and investment guides. These materials can be passed on to you through your trusted contacts. Make sure to ask for content that is beginner-friendly, given your current level of understanding. This will help you build your knowledge base and gradually become more confident in your investment decisions.

6. Legal and Ethical Considerations:

IT'S IMPORTANT TO ENSURE THAT ALL ACTIVITIES ARE conducted legally and ethically. Your trusted contacts should maintain clear records of all communications and transactions. They should also seek legal advice to ensure compliance with prison regulations and financial laws.

BY LEVERAGING THE KNOWLEDGE AND EXPERTISE OF FINANCIAL advisors through your trusted contacts, you can make more informed investment decisions and progress in your journey towards becoming a savvy investor—even from within the prison system. Remember, the key to success in investing is continuous learning and staying informed, and having a professional advisor can significantly facilitate this process.

Legal Considerations for Inmate Investors

"Legal considerations for incarcerated investors are not just about navigating regulations; they're about redefining access to financial empowerment within the confines of justice."
Unknown

Understanding Prison Regulations on Financial Activities

BEFORE DIVING INTO THE STOCK MARKET, IT'S ESSENTIAL TO grasp the rules and regulations governing financial activities within the prison system. Every facility has its own set of policies and understanding these guidelines will ensure that you remain compliant while pursuing your investment goals from behind bars.

. . .

Use of Outside Assistants

As previously discussed, due to restrictions on direct access to the internet and transactional capabilities, inmate investors require the assistance of someone outside the facility to manage various tasks. This could be a trusted family member, friend, or a professional financial advisor.

Communication Channels

In most prisons, inmates can communicate via phone calls, letters, or emails (subject to monitoring). When discussing financial plans or directives with your assistant, ensure that you're fully aware of any policies regarding these communications. Some prisons may have specific restrictions on the types of conversations permitted, so clarifying these rules beforehand will help avoid any violations.

Financial Accounts and Proxy Use

Typically, inmates are not allowed to open brokerage accounts or conduct stock transactions directly. Instead, your assistant will need to set up and manage these accounts on your behalf. This arrangement means you must provide clear, lawful instructions on how you want your money invested. It's advisable to formalize this instruction through a power of attorney, detailing your trusted assistant's responsibilities and limitations in managing your investments.

MONITORING AND REPORTING

PRISON FACILITIES MIGHT MONITOR ANY MONEY TRANSFERS OR financial activities involving inmates to prevent illicit transactions or money laundering. Ensure all transfers between you and your outside assistant for investment purposes are transparent, documented, and justifiable. Keeping records of these communications and transactions will help if you need to explain your activities to prison authorities.

COMPLIANCE WITH FEDERAL AND STATE LAWS

APART FROM PRISON REGULATIONS, FEDERAL AND STATE LAWS governing financial activities and investment must be adhered to. This includes tax obligations, reporting requirements, and ensuring your investment activities do not breach any laws. Your outside assistant can help you stay informed about these legal responsibilities.

Ethical Considerations

Besides legal compliance, ethical conduct is paramount. Engage in investment activities transparently and ethically. Avoid schemes that promise quick, high returns, as these are often scams. Education and due diligence are your best defenses against fraudulent opportunities.

Seeking Guidance

For inmates new to investing, consulting with a financial professional can be incredibly beneficial. They can provide tailored advice and help navigate both the investment landscape and the intricacies of managing investments from within a correctional facility.

By comprehensively understanding prison regulations on financial activities and cooperating closely with a trusted outside assistant, you can lay a solid foundation for your investment pursuits, ensuring they are lawful, ethical, and potentially rewarding, even from within prison walls.

SEEKING APPROVAL FROM PRISON AUTHORITIES FOR Investing

NAVIGATING THE COMPLEXITIES OF THE STOCK MARKET IS challenging enough, but as an incarcerated individual, you face additional hurdles that must be cleared, not least of which is obtaining permission from prison authorities. Here's a step-by-step guide to understanding and seeking this crucial approval.

1. Understand the Rules and Regulations:

EVERY CORRECTIONAL FACILITY OPERATES UNDER A DISTINCT set of rules and regulations. These guidelines can vary widely not only from state to state but also between federal and state institutions. It's essential to first familiarize yourself with the specific rules governing your current facility. The best way to do this is to consult the inmate handbook provided upon your arrival. If this document is unavailable, request it from a prison counselor or the administration office.

2. Identify Relevant Authorities:

IN MOST PRISONS, THE AUTHORITY TO GRANT PERMISSION FOR activities like investing will likely be a combination of the prison warden, a case manager, and the legal department. Understanding the hierarchy and identifying who needs to approve your request is critical.

4. Drafting a Request Letter:

A FORMAL WRITTEN REQUEST IS OFTEN NECESSARY. HERE'S A recommended structure for your request letter:

- *Introduction:* Start with your full name, inmate number, and the facility you're housed in. Clearly state your intention to engage in stock market investments.

- *Explanation:* Elaborate on why you want to invest, how it can be a part of your rehabilitation process, and the benefits it could bring in terms of financial literacy and management.
- *External Assistance:* Mention that, since direct access to trading platforms is restricted, you will be using an outside assistant. Detail how this person will manage your investments and ensure compliance with all legal requirements.
- *Compliance Assurance:* Assure them that all activities will be conducted within the framework of prison regulations and the law.

HERE IS A SAMPLE DRAFT:

[YOUR NAME]
  [Inmate Number]
  [Facility Name]
  [Date]

DEAR *[WARDEN/CASE MANAGER'S NAME]*,

. . .

I AM WRITING TO FORMALLY SEEK APPROVAL TO ENGAGE IN STOCK market investments while serving my sentence. I believe that this endeavor can significantly benefit my financial literacy and rehabilitative efforts, helping me to develop skills that will be valuable upon my release.

GIVEN THE CONSTRAINTS OF MY CURRENT CIRCUMSTANCES, I PLAN to enlist the aid of an external assistant who will manage my trades and ensure all activities comply with both legal standards and the regulations of this institution.

I ASSURE YOU THAT ALL TRANSACTIONS WILL BE TRANSPARENT AND subject to any oversight that you may deem necessary.

THANK YOU FOR CONSIDERING MY REQUEST.

SINCERELY,

[YOUR NAME]

4. Submit and Follow Up:

Submit your letter according to the facility's processes. This could involve handing it directly to your case manager or submitting it through an internal mail system. After submission, follow up regularly but respectfully. Patience is crucial as processing times can vary.

5. Meeting Compliance Requirements:

If permission is granted, you will need to continuously meet all compliance requirements established by prison authorities. This could include regular updates on your investment activities and ensuring that all trades are transparent and documented.

Remember, every interaction with prison authorities is an opportunity to demonstrate your commitment to constructive personal development. Being polite, prepared, and respectful significantly increases your chances of receiving a favorable response.

. . .

IN SUMMARY, OBTAINING APPROVAL TO INVEST WHILE incarcerated entails understanding your facility's regulations, drafting a comprehensive request, submitting it properly, and complying with any conditions set forth by the authorities. With the right approach and persistence, you can pave the way toward becoming a successful inmate investor.

COMPLIANCE WITH TAX LAWS AND REPORTING REQUIREMENTS

INVESTING IN THE STOCK MARKET COMES WITH ITS SET OF legal responsibilities, one of the most important being compliance with tax laws and reporting requirements. Whether you're inside or outside prison, it's critical to comply with these laws to avoid penalties, fines, or even additional legal issues. Here, we will break down what you need to know about tax compliance and how you can effectively manage these responsibilities even while incarcerated.

UNDERSTANDING TAXABLE EVENTS

. . .

WHEN YOU INVEST IN THE STOCK MARKET, CERTAIN ACTIVITIES can trigger what is known as "taxable events." These activities may include:

1. *Buying and Selling Stocks:* When you sell stocks for a profit or a loss, you must report this on your tax return. The profit is known as a capital gain, while a loss can offset other gains.
2. *Earning Dividends:* If you receive dividends from your stock investments, these are usually considered taxable income.
3. *Interest Income:* Any interest earned from investments is also subject to taxes.

IT'S IMPORTANT TO BE AWARE OF THESE EVENTS BECAUSE failing to report them correctly can result in penalties.

UTILIZING AN OUTSIDE ASSISTANT

AS AN INCARCERATED INDIVIDUAL, MANAGING AND REPORTING your investments can be challenging. This is where having an outside assistant can be invaluable. Your assistant can:

. . .

1. *Keep Track of Transactions:* They can maintain records of buying and selling stocks, dividends received, and any interest earned.
2. *Coordinate with a Tax Professional:* They can work with a tax preparer or accountant to ensure that all necessary documents are filled out accurately and submitted on time.
3. *File Tax Returns:* Your assistant can file your tax return on your behalf, ensuring that you meet all deadlines and comply with federal and state tax laws.

IMPORTANT FORMS AND DEADLINES

SEVERAL TAX FORMS AND DEADLINES ARE CRUCIAL FOR investors:

1. *Form 1099-B:* This form reports the proceeds from broker transactions. If you sell stocks, your broker will provide this form, detailing the sale price and dates.

2. *Form 1099-DIV:* This form reports dividends and distributions. If you receive dividends, your broker will issue this form.

3. *Form 1040:* This is the standard U.S. tax return form, where you'll report your investment income, capital gains, and other taxable events.

Taxes for the previous year are generally due by April 15. However, extensions can be filed if more time is needed.

Strategies for Simplifying Tax Compliance

1. *Automated Record-Keeping:* Leveraging financial software that your outside assistant can use to streamline record-keeping and minimize errors.

2. *Regular Reviews:* Periodically reviewing your investment transactions and taxable events with your assistant and tax professional ensures that you stay ahead of reporting requirements.

3. *Proactive Tax Planning:* Taking steps to minimize taxes, such as utilizing loss-harvesting strategies (selling stocks at a loss to offset gains), can be beneficial.

. . .

CONCLUSION

Adhering to tax laws and reporting requirements is a vital part of being a successful investor. By understanding taxable events, utilizing an outside assistant, and staying informed about important forms and deadlines, you can effectively manage your investment responsibilities even while incarcerated. Always remember, compliance isn't just a legal formality—it's an integral part of securing your financial future and maintaining your freedom when you return to society.

Overcoming Challenges and Limitations

"Challenges are what make life interesting, and overcoming them is
what makes life meaningful."
John C. Maxwell

Dealing with Limited Access to Information and Resources

INVESTING IN THE STOCK MARKET WHILE INCARCERATED presents unique challenges, particularly when it comes to accessing information and resources. However, these obstacles, though formidable, can be navigated with creativity, persistence, and the support of an outside assistant. This section will break down specific strategies and steps to ensure you can make informed investment decisions despite these limitations.

I. UTILIZING YOUR OUTSIDE ASSISTANT EFFECTIVELY

THE KEY TO OVERCOMING LIMITED ACCESS IS LEVERAGING THE support of an outside assistant effectively. This person should be someone you trust, who is willing to dedicate time to help you navigate the stock market. Here's how you can make the most of their assistance:

- *Information Relay:* Instruct your assistant to regularly send you printouts or summaries of stock market news, trends, and analysis. They can utilize sources like financial websites (e.g., Yahoo Finance, Bloomberg, MarketWatch), newsletters, and investment blogs.
  - *Correspondence:* Set up a structured schedule for regular correspondence (letters, phone calls, emails) where your assistant can provide updates and address any questions or investment ideas you may propose.

2. MAKING USE OF AVAILABLE PRISON RESOURCES

WHILE ACCESS WITHIN THE PRISON MAY BE LIMITED, THERE ARE still valuable resources that can aid your investment journey:

- *Library:* Prison libraries often have a selection of financial books and newspapers. Titles like "The Intelligent Investor" by Benjamin Graham or "One Up On Wall Street" by Peter Lynch can provide fundamental insights. Request these specific titles if they are not already available.
  - *Educational Programs:* Enquire about any business or finance-related courses available through the prison's education department. These programs can enhance your understanding of investment principles and financial literacy.

3. BUILDING A NETWORK OF KNOWLEDGE

CONNECTING WITH FELLOW INMATES WHO SHARE YOUR

interest in investing can create a mutually beneficial learning environment:

- *Study Groups:* Form a study group where you can discuss investment strategies, share insights from books or articles, and keep each other motivated.
  - *Mentorship:* Seek out inmates who have prior experience in finance or investing. Their knowledge can be invaluable, providing real-world insights that go beyond theoretical learning.

4. STAYING INFORMED THROUGH INDIRECT MEANS

DESPITE THE PHYSICAL LIMITATIONS, THERE ARE INDIRECT methods to stay informed:

- *Phone Access:* Use your phone privileges wisely. Have scheduled calls with your assistant specifically for investment discussions. Outline clear agendas for these calls to maximize the utility of the limited time.

- *Published Materials:* Magazines, journals, and investment newsletters mailed to you can be an ongoing source of information. Examples include "The Wall Street Journal," "Barron's," and "Forbes." Ensure to manage any associated costs and prerequisites for receiving these materials.

5. Tailoring Investment Choices to Your Situation

Given the constraints, consider investment options that require less frequent monitoring and are well-suited to a long-term strategy:

- *Index Funds and ETFs:* These options provide broad market exposure and typically require less hands-on management compared to individual stocks.
  - *Dividend Stocks:* Companies that consistently pay dividends can offer a potentially stable income stream, providing returns even during periods when market access or information is limited.

. . .

By creatively utilizing the resources available to you and effectively leveraging the support structure provided by an outside assistant and your prison environment, you can navigate the challenges of limited access to information and resources. The path might be more complex, but with determination and strategic planning, your goal of becoming a knowledgeable and successful investor is well within reach.

Managing Investments Without Direct Control

One of the most significant challenges you will face as an incarcerated investor is managing your investments without having direct access to online trading platforms, bank accounts, or other necessary financial tools. While this may seem like a lot, it is entirely possible with careful planning and the right support network.

1. Appointing a Trusted Assistant:

Since you cannot directly execute trades or manage your investment portfolio, you will need someone outside prison—a trusted assistant—to act on your behalf. This assistant can be a family member, a close friend, or even a professional financial advisor. The most important criterion is trustworthiness, as they will have significant control over your financial resources. Make sure they are fully aware of your investment goals and strategies. I know this may seem repetitive at this point, but a trusted outside assistant is just that much a major part of what needs to be done.

2. POWER OF ATTORNEY:

To LEGALLY AUTHORIZE YOUR ASSISTANT TO MANAGE YOUR investments, you'll need to grant them Power of Attorney (POA). A *POA* is a legal document that allows someone to make decisions and take actions on your behalf. There are various types of POA but a durable Power of Attorney for financial matters will be most suited to your needs. Consult with a legal advisor to properly draft this document to ensure it provides the necessary authority while protecting your interests.

3. ESTABLISHING CLEAR COMMUNICATION:

. . .

CLEAR AND REGULAR COMMUNICATION BETWEEN YOU AND YOUR assistant is crucial. Set up a schedule for discussing your investment strategy, reviewing portfolio performance, and making decisions about buying or selling stocks. Letters, scheduled phone calls, and even email (if accessible) can be used for this purpose. Keeping records of all communications is also beneficial for future reference.

4. CREATING A ROBUST INVESTMENT PLAN:

BEFORE YOUR ASSISTANT BEGINS MANAGING YOUR INVESTMENTS, develop a detailed investment plan. This plan should outline your financial goals, risk tolerance, preferred investment types, and any specific assets or sectors you want to focus on. The more detailed your plan, the easier it will be for your assistant to make decisions that align with your objectives.

5. MONITORING PERFORMANCE:

THOUGH YOU WON'T HAVE DIRECT ACCESS TO YOUR INVESTMENT accounts, you can still monitor their performance through regular updates from your assistant. Request periodic reports outlining the performance of your investments, including any changes that were made and why. This will help you stay informed and make necessary adjustments to your strategy.

6. CONTINGENCY PLANNING:

PREPARE FOR UNEXPECTED SITUATIONS BY ESTABLISHING contingency plans. What happens if your assistant is no longer available or able to manage your investments? Have a backup person in mind and ensure they are familiar with your investment plan and goals. Additionally, consider setting up alerts or notifications on your accounts to flag significant activities or changes, ensuring you remain informed even if things go off track.

7. EDUCATION AND RESOURCES:

YOUR ASSISTANT DOESN'T NEED TO BE A FINANCIAL EXPERT, BUT they should have a basic understanding of investing and the stock market. Provide them with educational resources, such as books, online courses, and articles that can help them become more knowledgeable. Furthermore, encourage them to consult with a professional financial advisor if they encounter complex investment decisions.

. . .

BY EFFECTIVELY LEVERAGING THE ASSISTANCE OF A TRUSTED individual and employing strategies to maintain oversight and communication, you can successfully manage your investments even without direct control. This approach will enable you to stay connected to your financial goals, build your investment portfolio, and work towards financial stability despite the constraints of your current environment.

STRATEGIES FOR OVERCOMING COMMUNICATION BARRIERS WITH the outside world

FOR INCARCERATED INDIVIDUALS AIMING TO NAVIGATE THE stock market, one of the primary challenges is overcoming communication barriers with the outside world. This is especially critical when you need an outside assistant to handle certain tasks that can't be managed from inside the prison. Here are some practical strategies to ensure smooth and effective communication with your outside assistant:

1. **Establish Clear Communication Channels:**
   - *Phone Calls:* Use the available phone call system to maintain regular contact. Although

call times may be limited, make each call count by having a clear agenda. List out topics or questions beforehand to ensure you cover everything important.

- o *Emails and Letters:* Writing can be a powerful tool. Detailed letters or emails can lay out your investment strategies or instructions clearly. Be specific about what actions need to be taken by your assistant.
- o *Scheduled Visits:* Maximize the potential of scheduled visits. Use them to discuss complex strategies that may be difficult to convey over phone calls or letters. Prepare written notes or questions to utilize the time effectively.

2. **Utilize a Trusted Network:**
   - o *Identify a Reliable Assistant:* Choose someone you trust implicitly. This person will be your conduit to the financial world. Discuss your overall objectives and ensure they understand your goals and investment strategies.
   - o *Set Up Regular Updates:* Establish a schedule for your assistant to provide you with regular updates on your investment portfolio. This could be weekly or monthly, depending on

your investment strategy and how often you
can communicate.

3. **Educate and Delegate:**
   - *Empower Your Assistant:* Your assistant should
     have a strong understanding of basic
     investment principles. Provide them with
     learning resources or guide them to online
     courses that align with your investment
     strategy.
   - *Delegate Wisely:* Clearly outline which
     decisions your assistant can make
     independently and which ones require your
     input. For instance, they might be able to
     handle buying and selling stocks within
     certain parameters but need your approval for
     major changes.

4. **Leverage Available Resources:**
   - *Prison Library and Workshops:* Maximize the
     use of books and any available educational
     resources within the prison to stay updated
     and strategize effectively.

○ *Third-Party Services:* There are organizations dedicated to helping incarcerated individuals stay connected with outside activities. Research and utilize such services to facilitate smoother communication.

5. USE TECHNOLOGY WHERE POSSIBLE:

- *Online Platforms:* If access to internet or digital financial tools is available, use these platforms to track your investments and stay informed. Provide your assistant with access to these accounts where safe and permissible.
  ○ *Investment Simulations:* Some prisons may have access to investment simulation tools. Use these to practice and refine your strategies.

6. DOCUMENT EVERYTHING:

- *Keep Detailed Records:* Maintain a record of all communications and decisions. This will help in tracking progress, making informed decisions, and resolving any potential misunderstandings.

- o *Legal Considerations:* Be aware of legal restrictions and ensure all transactions and communications comply with prison regulations.

BY FOCUSING ON THESE STRATEGIES, YOU CAN CREATE AN effective communication framework that keeps you connected with the outside world, allowing you to make informed investment decisions and successfully manage your portfolio from behind bars.

Case Studies and Success Stories

"Success is not final, failure is not fatal: It is the courage to continue that counts."
Winston Churchill

Real-life Examples of Successful Inmate Investors

Even in the challenging environment of prison, some inmates have managed to become successful investors, proving that it's possible to achieve financial success despite significant barriers. These real-life examples can serve as powerful inspiration, demonstrating that determination, knowledge, and strategic planning can lead to fruitful investing. Here are a few notable stories:

Michael Santos

Michael Santos served 26 years in federal prison for drug-related charges. During his incarceration, he focused on education and self-improvement, including learning about finance and investing. One of his primary strategies was leveraging the help of an outside assistant. Michael regularly communicated with his wife, who executed his investment decisions based on the research and strategies he formulated.

By carefully studying market trends and making informed decisions, Michael was able to earn a substantial amount of money through stock investments. He often chose to invest in index funds, which provided broad market exposure and reduced the risk associated with individual stock picks. Upon his release, he had a solid financial foundation, which allowed him to rebuild his life more seamlessly.

Curtis "Wall Street" Carroll

Curtis Carroll, also known as "Wall Street," is another remarkable example. Curtis was illiterate when he entered prison but taught himself to read and later developed a profound interest in stocks and the financial market. Utilizing the prison library and any financial materials he could find, Curtis became knowledgeable about investing. He made his initial investments through an outside assistant who acted on his instructions.

Curtis focused on long-term investments in companies he believed had strong growth potential. He emphasized the importance of understanding the companies he invested in, their management, and market competition. His disciplined approach to investing earned him significant returns, and he became a mentor to other inmates. His success is now well-documented, and he is a sought-after speaker on financial literacy and investment strategies.

Richard Wershe, Jr.

Known as "White Boy Rick," Richard Wershe, Jr. was involved in the drug trade as a teenager before being incarcerated for many years. While in prison, he became intrigued by the stock market and began educating himself about investments. With the help of family members on the outside, Richard was able to channel his knowledge into practical investing.

Richard took a diversified approach, investing in a mix of stocks, bonds, and mutual funds. This diversification helped mitigate the risks and stabilize his returns over the years. By consistently educating himself and making prudent investment decisions, Richard built a portfolio that provided financial security and opportunities for his family.

Key Takeaways

From these stories, several key lessons can be learned:

1. *Initiate with Education:* Each successful inmate investor took the time to educate themselves thoroughly. They utilized available resources, whether it was the prison library, books, or financial publications.

2. *Leverage Outside Assistance:* Having a trusted person outside to execute trades and manage accounts was crucial. This highlights the importance of communication and trust with the outside assistant.

3. *Adopt a Long-term Vision:* The most common thread among these investors was a focus on long-term gains rather than short-term profits. They selected investments that promised steady, reliable growth.

4. *Diversification:* By spreading investments across various asset classes and sectors, they mitigated the risk and enhanced the stability of their returns.

5. *Continuous Learning:* The financial world is constantly evolving and staying updated with the latest trends and strategies was key to their success.

These real-life examples show that with the right mindset, education, and strategy, it is possible to become a successful investor even from within the confines of a prison.

Lessons Learned from Their Experiences

Drawing inspiration from the success stories of inmates

like Michael Santos, Curtis "Wall Street" Carroll, and Richard Wershe, Jr., we can extract valuable lessons that can guide aspiring investors currently in prison. These lessons distill the core strategies and mindsets that contributed to their financial success despite significant barriers.

1. Commit to Continuous Education

A recurring theme among successful inmate investors is a commitment to self-education. Here's how you can implement this lesson:

- *Utilize Available Resources:* Maximize the use of the prison library. Seek out books on investing, financial markets, and personal finance.
    - *Follow Financial News:* If possible, subscribe to financial newspapers or magazines to stay abreast of market trends and developments.
    - *Study Success Stories:* Learn from other investors by reading their biographies or case studies. This can offer insights and strategies that you can adapt to your own situation.

2. Build a Trustworthy Support Network

Having a trusted individual on the outside to execute trades and manage investments is crucial. Here are key steps to ensure effective collaboration:

- *Choose Wisely:* Select someone you trust completely, whether a family member, a close friend, or a legal advisor.
  - *Communicate Clearly:* Ensure clear, consistent communication. Share your investment decisions, research, and strategies in a detailed manner.
  - *Keep Them Informed:* Encourage your assistant to stay informed about the stock market so they can effectively carry out your plans.

3. Develop a Long-term Investment Strategy

Successful investors often focus on the long term rather than seeking quick wins. Here's how you can adopt a long-term perspective:

- *Research Thoroughly:* Invest time in understanding the companies you plan to invest in. Look at their financial health, management teams, competitive advantages, and market prospects.
  - Avoid Speculation: Resist the temptation to engage in speculative trading, which can be highly risky and is akin to gambling.
  - *Think Big Picture:* Aim to build a diversified portfolio that will grow steadily over the years, providing a more secure financial future.

4. Practice Diversification

Diversification reduces risk and enhances the stability of your investment portfolio. Here's how to put this into practice:

- *Spread Investments:* Don't put all your money into one stock or one type of investment. Spread your investments across various sectors and asset classes, such as stocks, bonds, and mutual funds.
  - *Balance Risk and Reward:* Mix high-risk, high-reward investments with more stable, secure ones. This balance can protect you from substantial losses during market downturns.

5. Maintain Discipline and Patience

Successful investing often requires emotional discipline and patience. Here's how you can cultivate these traits:

- *Set Clear Goals:* Have specific, measurable financial goals. This gives you something to work towards and helps you stay focused.
  - *Avoid Emotional Decisions:* Market fluctuations are normal. Stick to your research and long-term strategy rather than making impulsive decisions based on short-term market movements.

○ *Stay the Course:* Understand that building wealth through investing is a marathon, not a sprint. Be prepared to stay invested for the long haul.

6. Leverage Available Technology and Tools

While access to technology may be limited, there are ways to leverage what you do have:

- *Paper Trade:* Practice trading on paper before making real trades. This helps you test strategies without risking actual money.
  - ○ *Use Dictionaries and Manuals:* Study investment terminology and manuals to familiarize yourself with the language and concepts of the stock market.

7. Foster a Positive Mindset

Believing in your ability to succeed despite your current circumstances is crucial. Here's how to maintain a positive mindset:

- *Stay Motivated:* Remember that many have walked this path before you and succeeded. Let their stories motivate and inspire you.
  - ○ *Celebrate Small Wins:* Recognize and celebrate your small achievements along the way. This

will help you stay motivated and focused on your larger goals.

- o *Stay Resilient:* Understand that setbacks are part of the journey. Learn from your mistakes and keep moving forward with determination.

CONCLUSION

By learning from the experiences of successful inmate investors, you can chart your own path to financial success. Remember, it takes education, strategic planning, discipline, and a supportive network to navigate the complexities of the stock market from prison. These lessons can serve as a roadmap, helping you make informed decisions and steadily build your financial future.

Inspirational Stories to Motivate Readers

The journey of investing from prison can seem daunting, but the success stories of those who've walked this path before you prove that it is possible. Here, we'll share some additional inspirational stories to ignite your motivation and reinforce the idea that with determination, education, and strategic planning, you too can achieve financial success.

Andre Norman: Transforming Adversity into Triumph

Andre Norman's journey is one of remarkable transformation. Growing up in a violent neighborhood and becoming involved in crime led him to a life of incarceration.

However, Andre refused to let prison define his future. He dedicated himself to self-improvement, learning to read, and expanding his knowledge.

While Andre's primary focus was on personal development and education, his transformative journey included understanding the importance of financial literacy. His story exemplifies how a change in mindset and commitment to learning can lay the groundwork for future financial success. Upon his release, Andre became a motivational speaker, guiding others towards making positive changes in their lives. His story underscores the powerful impact of resilience and self-belief.

Tihar Jail's Investment Success

In Tihar Jail, one of the largest prisons in Asia, a unique initiative was launched to teach inmates about stock market investing. The program started when a handful of inmates expressed interest in learning about finance. One particular inmate, Ram, who was serving a life sentence, took a keen interest in the lessons.

Ram diligently studied investment principles, market trends, and financial analysis. With assistance from the prison's partnership with local financial institutions, he executed investment strategies. His first few trades yielded positive results, encouraging more inmates to participate. Over time, Ram's portfolio grew impressively, and he used his earnings to support his family outside.

Tihar Jail's program demonstrated that structured education and support could transform inmates into successful investors. The initiative reduced recidivism by providing inmates with financial stability and a sense of purpose.

Chris Wilson: The Master Plan

Chris Wilson grew up in a challenging environment with few opportunities. A series of unfortunate events led to his incarceration, but Chris was determined to turn his life around. He created what he called "The Master Plan," a detailed roadmap for personal development, education, and future success.

Chris included financial learning in his Master Plan, educating himself on investment principles. He wrote letters to financial experts who provided guidance and feedback. With the help of an outside assistant, he made strategic investments that grew significantly over time.

Upon his release, Chris wrote a memoir titled, "The Master Plan," to share his journey and inspire others. He now runs a successful social enterprise that helps former inmates reintegrate into society and achieve financial independence.

John Lee Dumas: Navy Veteran Turned Financial Guru

John Lee Dumas, although not an inmate, faced his own set of challenges when transitioning from a military career to civilian life. Struggling with purpose and direction, he eventually found solace in understanding personal finance and investing.

John dedicated himself to learning everything he could

about the stock market, often reading into the early hours of the morning. His tenacity paid off when he began a podcast, *Entrepreneur on Fire,* where he shared financial advice and inspirational interviews, including stories of those who had successfully invested from prison.

By offering platforms where inmate investors could share their experiences, John played a pivotal role in bringing their stories to the forefront, inspiring many to believe in their potential to succeed despite their circumstances.

Practical Steps from Their Stories

Here are some practical steps you can take from these inspirational stories:

- *Create a Personal Development Plan:* Outline your goals, both personal and financial. Break them into achievable steps and track your progress.
- *Seek Educational Resources:* Utilize available resources to educate yourself. Write to experts if possible and seek external guidance and mentorship.
- *Maintain a Positive Mindset:* Draw inspiration from these stories to stay motivated. Remember that your current circumstances do not define your future.
- *Network and Collaborate:* Build a support system both inside and outside the prison. Collaboration can open doors to new opportunities.

- *Focus on the Long Term:* Be patient and committed to your goals. Long-term planning and consistency are key to achieving financial success.

CONCLUSION

These inspirational stories highlight the incredible potential for transformation and success, even from within the confines of prison. Let them motivate you to pursue your financial goals with determination and resilience. With the right mindset, education, and strategic planning, you can write your own success story and pave the way for a brighter financial future.

The New Faces of Black Financial Literacy

One of the greatest ways to learn about investing is to see the journeys and successes of those who have walked the path before you. In this sub-section, we focus on influential figures in the Black community who have made significant strides in promoting financial literacy. These individuals serve as powerful examples of how anyone, regardless of their circumstances, can become knowledgeable and successful in investing. Let's break down the stories and contributions of some key figures in the Black Financial Literacy space:

The Wallstreet Trapper

Wallstreet Trapper, whose real name is Leon Howard, is a

motivational financial educator known for his work in teaching people, particularly those from underserved communities, about investing and financial literacy. His story is quite compelling and inspirational.

Leon Howard grew up in New Orleans in an environment surrounded by crime and poverty. By the age of 16, he found himself incarcerated for a total of 10 years. It was during his time in prison that he realized he needed to make a significant change in his life to break the cycle of poverty and crime.

Howard's turning point came when a prison employee introduced him to the concepts of the stock market and investing. Fascinated by the idea that he could build wealth legally, he began dedicating his time to learning everything he could about the financial markets. After his release, he continued his education in finance and started to apply his knowledge to build his own financial security.

Leon Howard adopted the moniker "Wallstreet Trapper" and began using social media platforms and public speaking engagements to share his knowledge and experiences. Through his content, he aims to demystify the stock market and investment strategies for individuals who might feel intimidated or excluded from these financial spaces. His focus is on empowering people to take control of their financial future by offering practical advice, relatable anecdotes, and easy-to-understand explanations of complex financial concepts.

Wallstreet Trapper's story is a powerful testament to personal transformation and the impact of financial education. By leveraging his own experiences, he has become a significant advocate for financial literacy and economic empowerment, particularly within communities that have traditionally been overlooked by the mainstream financial industry.

Aristotle Investments

Aristotle Investments is an online persona and brand created by Brandon Leake, who has gained popularity on Instagram and other social media platforms by sharing content related to stock market investing, financial education, and personal finance tips. He uses the nickname "Aristotle" to convey wisdom and knowledge in the realm of investing, inspired by the famous Greek philosopher, Aristotle.

Brandon Leake's story is one of entrepreneurial success and a commitment to financial education. He has built a significant following by breaking down complex financial concepts into easily understandable and actionable advice. His engaging content appeals to a broad audience, particularly younger individuals who are interested in learning about the stock market and achieving financial independence.

Leake often shares his own experiences, strategies, and insights into investing, aiming to demystify the stock market and help others make informed financial decisions. Through his platform, he offers educational resources, courses, and other tools to help individuals build wealth and navigate the world of investing.

If you're interested in learning more about Aristotle Investments or Brandon Leake's content, you can visit his Instagram page or other social media profiles where he actively engages with his audience and provides regular updates and educational materials.

Dream Green Show

Dream Green Show, hosted and operated by an investor known as Zeke, is a content creator on YouTube who focuses primarily on topics related to finance, investing, and passive income. His channel aims to educate viewers on how to make smart financial decisions, manage their money, and build wealth over time through various investment strategies. Zeke covers a range of topics, including stock market investing, real estate, dividend investing, and other methods to generate passive income streams.

Zeke's story is one of personal growth and financial education. He often shares his own experiences, successes, and lessons learned along the way to becoming financially independent. Through transparent and informative videos, he hopes to inspire others to take control of their financial futures. His content is designed to be accessible to people at all stages of their financial journeys, whether they are just starting out or are seasoned investors.

If you're interested in improving your financial literacy or looking for practical investment advice, Dream Green Show might be a valuable resource to consider.

Chris Sain

Chris Sain, a widely recognized figure in the world of investing and personal finance, rose to prominence through his insightful financial guidance and investment strategies, particularly in the realm of the stock market. His journey is not just inspiring but also a testament to the power of leveraging knowledge and technology to achieve financial independence.

Chris Sain's story starts in Detroit, Michigan, where he grew up before embarking on a journey that would make him a notable finance influencer and mentor. He has often shared his beginnings in a humble environment and how those early life challenges shaped his approach to finance and investing. What sets Chris apart is not just his knack for picking promising stocks, especially in the growing sectors like technology and biotech, but also his commitment to educating others. He's well-known for his straightforward, accessible advice that appeals to both beginners and seasoned investors.

Beyond stock picks, Chris focuses on broader financial well-being, advocating for income diversification, debt management, and wealth-building strategies that are inclusive and accessible. This holistic approach to personal finance, combined with his engaging communication style, has amassed a significant following on social media platforms and YouTube, where he shares his insights and investment philosophies.

His work goes beyond individual gains; Chris Sain is dedicated to fostering a community where knowledge about wealth creation and financial health is open and shared freely. He often emphasizes the importance of starting your investment journey as early as possible, highlighting the benefits of compounding and strategic risk-taking.

Chris Sain's story is not just about personal success in the stock market; it's a beacon for many who aspire to achieve financial independence and literacy. Through his efforts, he embodies the principle that with the right knowledge and tools, anyone can navigate the complex world of investing and secure a prosperous future.

Jeffrey Williams

Jeffery Williams, often referred to as "Stock Chart Shawty," is an entrepreneur and social media personality known for his insights and expertise in trading and stock market analysis. He gained popularity through his engaging content on platforms like Instagram, where he shares stock tips, trading strategies, and educational material for both novice and experienced traders.

His story is one of resilience and self-education. Coming from a background where financial literacy was not emphasized, Williams took it upon himself to learn about investing and the stock market. Over time, he developed his own strategies and began to share his journey online. His down-to-earth approach and ability to break down complex concepts into digestible content have resonated with many followers.

Through his platform, he encourages others to take control of their financial futures, emphasizing the importance of understanding the market and making informed decisions. His charismatic personality and relatable content have made him a prominent figure in the online trading community.

Ian Dunlap

Ian Dunlap, often recognized as "The Master Investor," is an entrepreneur, stock market investor, and financial educator. His rise to prominence is largely attributed to his expertise in the stock market and his ability to communicate complex financial concepts in an accessible manner. Through various platforms and public appearances, he has helped numerous individuals better understand investing and personal finance.

<u>Background and Career:</u>

- *Early Life:* Ian Dunlap's early life details are less publicized, but he often alludes to overcoming significant challenges and humble beginnings, which have fueled his drive to succeed and educate others.

- *Corporate America:* Before becoming a full-time investor and educator, Dunlap worked in corporate environments, gaining valuable insights and experience in business and finance.

- *Becoming "The Master Investor":* Over time, Dunlap honed his investment strategies and began sharing his knowledge through social media, podcasts, webinars, and live appearances. His practical advice and emphasis on discipline in investing have resonated with a broad audience.

Philosophy and Approach:

- *Financial Literacy:* Central to Ian Dunlap's mission is improving financial literacy, particularly among underrepresented communities. He advocates for a straightforward and disciplined approach to investing, emphasizing the importance of long-term strategies over get-rich-quick schemes.

- *Education:* His educational efforts include courses, seminars, and content that break down stock market concepts, investment strategies, and wealth-building tactics. He frequently challenges conventional financial advice and promotes independent thinking.

- *Community Building:* Dunlap has fostered a strong online community where individuals can share insights, ask questions, and support each other on their financial journeys. His active engagement with his audience has built a loyal following.

Public Appearances and Contributions:

- *Podcasts and Interviews:* Ian Dunlap has appeared on numerous financial podcasts and interviews, sharing his story and investment philosophy. His insights are often sought after by media outlets covering finance and economics.

- *Social Media:* He maintains a robust presence on platforms like Instagram, Twitter, and YouTube, where he shares market analysis, motivational content, and personal anecdotes.

- *Public Speaking:* Dunlap is also a dynamic public speaker, often delivering keynote addresses at financial conferences and events. He uses these opportunities to inspire and educate larger audiences.

Impact and Legacy:

Ian Dunlap's impact extends beyond mere financial gain;

he aims to empower people to achieve financial independence and security. His approachable teaching style and commitment to improving financial literacy make him a significant figure in today's financial education landscape.

While there may be some variability in his public perception—common for most public figures—Dunlap's dedication to educating others on investing and personal finance is well-regarded. If you're looking to improve your understanding of the stock market or personal finance, Ian Dunlap's resources could be a valuable starting point.

Earn Your Leisure

Earn Your Leisure is a media platform and podcast focused on financial literacy, entrepreneurship, and lifestyle. It was created by Rashad Bilal and Troy Millings, who are childhood friends with backgrounds in finance and education, respectively. The platform aims to break down complex financial concepts, share investment strategies, and highlight the stories of successful entrepreneurs and business leaders, particularly within the Black community.

Their story is built on a commitment to democratizing financial knowledge and making it accessible to a wider audience. They started their journey by hosting workshops and seminars in their local community but soon realized they could reach many more people by leveraging digital platforms. Thus, the "Earn Your Leisure" podcast was born.

The podcast has gained significant popularity, in part due to its engaging format and the duo's ability to distill complicated financial topics into easy-to-understand advice. The show features interviews with a diverse array of guests, including athletes, entertainers, and business moguls, who share their own financial journeys and the lessons they've learned along the way. This combination of sound advice and inspirational stories has resonated with audiences and helped to grow the "Earn Your Leisure" brand.

In addition to the podcast, *Earn Your Leisure* has expanded into other areas such as live events, educational courses, and a networking platform called "EYL University." Their mission remains focused on empowering individuals to take control of their financial futures and to build generational wealth.

These trailblazers have not only found success in the stock market themselves but have also dedicated their careers to educating and uplifting others. By following their stories and absorbing their wisdom, you can gain a deeper understanding of how to navigate the world of investing, even from within the prison system. Remember, financial literacy is a powerful tool, and with determination and the right resources, you can set the foundation for a successful investing journey.

I also want to add that they just recently released a new book January 14th 2025 titled, You Deserve to Be Rich: Master the Inner Game of Wealth and Claim Your Future. It has a 4.9 star rating on Amazon, and is said to be a very inspiring New York Times Bestseller. The book starts by focusing on mindset, which I really appreciated, because changing how you think about money is such an important first step.

I placed the synopsis below:

NEW YORK TIMES BESTSELLER • A revolutionary play-book for building generational wealth, no matter where you grew up—from the founders of the explosively popular podcast and financial literacy platform Earn Your Leisure

You deserve to be rich.

You deserve to make a purchase without fear that your check might bounce. You deserve to go on vacation. You deserve to care for loved ones without worrying about bills. You deserve to live the way you want, without reservations or fear. You deserve freedom —financial freedom. If you agree, you've come to the right place.

We grew up in New York playing basketball together. As kids, both of us were fascinated by finance, curious about the stock market, and how money moves among systems and pockets. But we began to notice that—for people in our community—hard work wasn't enough. The system wasn't set up to help people like us turn our hustle into lasting wealth.

We started Earn Your Leisure to change that. We never could have imagined the response. Soon our little podcast started to feel more like a financial revolution. But a podcast can do only so much. This book is our answer to the thousands upon thousands of people who have asked us for a detailed blueprint. The key to earning your leisure is to see money as a strategic tool for wealth development. In You Deserve to Be Rich, you'll learn how to:

• *Deal with the psychological toll of growing up living paycheck to paycheck.*

• *Create income-building strategies outside your nine-to-five, from investing to side hustles.*

• *Use passive income to put you in control of your time and lifestyle.*

• *Master tax and insurance systems and identify (legal) loopholes to maximize wealth.*

• *Navigate family financial drama and find ways to support your community.*

That's just the start. This book is full of tips, insights, and stories about real people, just like you, who have used the tools of wealth building to overcome barriers and build the life they want.

You deserve to be rich. This is the playbook to make it happen.

I've learned a lot from the advice my people have provided me through them so I don't mind promoting them in any way possible. It's enough for everyone to eat, and them eating takes nothing out of my mouth. This is definitely a book that yall want to read on yall financial journey.

Ethical Investing from Prison

"Every time you spend money, you're casting a vote for the kind of world you want."
Anna Lappé

Importance of Ethical Considerations in Investing

Investing ethically means making choices that align not just with potential financial returns but also with broader social, environmental, and governance concerns. Especially from within the prison system, where your resources and opportunities might be more limited, understanding and applying ethical investing principles can be particularly rewarding and impactful. Here's why ethical considerations in investing are important:

I. Aligning Investments with Personal Values

When you invest ethically, you're putting your money

into companies and industries that reflect your values and beliefs. For many, this means avoiding investments in businesses engaged in practices they find harmful, such as tobacco, firearms, or fossil fuels, and instead focusing on those advocating for positive change, like renewable energy, fair labor practices, or social justice initiatives. This alignment can give a greater sense of purpose and integrity to your investment journey.

2. Long-term Sustainability

Ethical investing often focuses on companies that are not only profitable but also sustainable and responsible. These companies usually have practices in place that ensure they can operate successfully in the long term without causing harm to the environment or society. This can make them more resilient to certain risks, like regulatory changes or social unrest, which might impact less ethical companies adversely. In the long run, this enhances the potential for stable returns on your investments.

3. Mitigating Risk

Investing in unethical or controversial companies can pose significant risks. For instance, a company involved in environmental pollution might face large fines, legal battles, and negative public sentiment, all of which can hurt its profitability and, consequently, your investment returns. Ethical investing helps mitigate these risks by steering clear of businesses that operate on shaky grounds.

4. Positive Social Impact

One of the most compelling reasons to invest ethically is the potential to drive positive change. By directing capital towards companies that act responsibly and sustainably, you support practices that benefit society as a whole. This can include initiatives like reducing carbon emissions, promoting gender equality, or creating fair labor conditions. Your investments can be a powerful tool for influencing the market towards more ethical conduct.

5. Growing Trend and Broader Acceptance

Ethical investing is not just a niche area; it's a growing trend globally. More and more investors and major financial institutions are recognizing the value of incorporating ethical considerations into their investment strategies. This broader acceptance means there are growing resources, tools, and markets available to support ethical investing. As an incarcerated individual looking to invest from prison, this is particularly advantageous since information and assistance from the outside can be more accessible when aligning with widely acknowledged practices.

6. Personal Satisfaction and Social Responsibility

There's a unique sense of satisfaction that comes from knowing your investments are contributing to a better world. By engaging in ethical investing, you are acting as a socially responsible individual, making conscious choices that reflect an understanding of your wider impact on the world. This sense of responsibility and integrity can be especially meaningful within the prison context, where opportunities to contribute positively to society might feel limited.

To sum it up, ethical investing represents a meaningful and potentially rewarding approach to managing your finances from prison. It involves a careful assessment of where your money goes and understanding the broader implications of your investment choices. By seeking help from an outside assistant, you can better navigate the complexities of the market, ensuring that your investments not only yield financial returns but also contribute positively to society and the environment.

Avoiding Investments in Controversial Industries or Companies

When you embark on the journey of ethical investing, you consciously choose to support businesses and industries that align with your personal values and morals. This means avoiding investments in controversial industries or companies, even if they might offer high returns. But what does this entail, and how can you make these choices while in prison? Let's break it down step by step.

1. **Understanding Controversial Industries:**

Controversial industries are sectors that often engage in activities that may be considered harmful to society, the environment, or ethical standards. Some examples include:

- *Tobacco:* Companies producing cigarettes and other tobacco products.

- *Alcohol:* Companies involved in the production and sale of alcoholic beverages.
- *Weapons and Firearms:* Businesses that manufacture and sell guns and other weapons.
- *Fossil Fuels:* Companies involved in the extraction, production, and sale of non-renewable energy sources like oil and coal.
- *Gambling:* Casinos and other gaming establishments.
- *Pornography:* Businesses involved in adult entertainment.

2. Recognizing Controversial Companies:

Even within generally positive industries, some companies may engage in practices that are deemed unethical, such as poor labor conditions, environmental damage, or corrupt business practices. Researching and identifying these companies is crucial.

3. Relying on Your Outside Assistant:

As an incarcerated individual, your internet access is limited, if available at all. This is where your outside assistant plays a crucial role. Here's how they can help:

- *Research:* Ask your assistant to look up companies and industries for you. Provide them with a list of sectors that you wish to avoid and let them do the research on whether specific companies fall under those categories.

- *Ethical Investment Platforms:* There are platforms and funds specifically designed for ethical investing, such as ESG (Environmental, Social, and Governance) funds. Your assistant can help you explore these options and may find lists of recommended companies.
- *Regular Updates:* Encourage your assistant to stay updated on current events. Companies can change their practices and new information might influence your investment decisions.

4. Using Exclusionary Screens:

An *exclusionary screen* is a tool used by investors to exclude certain sectors or companies from their investments. You can instruct your assistant to use exclusionary screens offered by various investment platforms to filter out controversial stocks. Here's how it works:

- *Prepare a List:* Make a list of industries and behaviors you want to exclude. Consult ethical investment guidelines, which often provide these lists.
- *Screening Tools:* Your assistant can use online tools that allow filtering investments based on ethical criteria. These tools are often available on

investment platforms, and some are specifically designed for ethical investors.

5. Utilizing Ethical Investment Services:

There are services available that specialize in ethical investments:

- *Robo-Advisors:* Some robo-advisors cater specifically to ethical investing. They automate the process, making it easier for you and your assistant to manage your portfolio in line with your ethical values.
- *Mutual Funds and ETFs:* Many mutual funds and Exchange-Traded Funds (ETFs) focus on ethical investing. These funds diversify your investments across numerous companies adhering to ethical standards.

6. Communicating Clearly:

Clear communication with your outside assistant is *essential*. Be explicit about your values and the types of investments you wish to avoid. Regularly review and reassess these criteria together to ensure your portfolio remains aligned with your ethical principles.

Choosing to avoid investments in controversial industries or companies is a powerful way to make a positive impact with your finances. Even from within prison, you can maintain a commitment to investing in a manner that aligns with your personal ethical standards, thanks to the assistance of someone on the outside who understands and supports your goals.

I was listening to Wallstreet Trapper speak one time, and he mentioned the fact that he didn't invest in prison stocks because they didn't align with his personal values. I second that. Never would I support something that has been one of the most oppressive systems to my race. Yet, Michael Jordan does. It's not a bad investment business wise. Don't get me wrong, prisons are necessary, and I imagine they would be a good investment because they'll always be around. Me investing my money into it, though? No. There are plenty of lucrative companies I can put my money into. All money ain't good money. You have to stand for something. That's the way I see it, anyways.

Making Socially Responsible Investment Choices

When you're considering investing in the stock market, it's essential to think beyond just making a profit. Ethical investing, also known as socially responsible investing (SRI), involves selecting investments that align with your personal values and contribute positively to society. This may seem challenging from prison, but with careful research and the right mindset, you can make investment choices that do good while potentially earning good returns.

What is Socially Responsible Investing (SRI)?

Socially responsible investing means choosing stocks,

bonds, or other investments that are not only profitable but also ethical. Ethical investments avoid companies engaging in harmful practices like environmental degradation, exploitation, or unethical labor practices. Instead, they favor businesses that contribute positively to society, such as those promoting sustainable environmental practices, social justice, and ethical governance.

Steps to Make Socially Responsible Investment Choices

1. *Identify Your Values:* Before you start investing, it's crucial to reflect on your values. Ask yourself what's important to you. Do you care deeply about the environment, mass incarceration, human rights, or fair labor practices? Your investments should reflect these principles.

2. *Research Companies:* Once you've identified your values, research companies that align with them. Look for businesses with strong records in corporate social responsibility (CSR), environmentally friendly practices, or fair labor policies.

3. *Use SRI Funds:* If researching individual companies seems overwhelming, consider socially responsible investment funds. These are

mutual funds or exchange-traded funds (ETFs) that pool money from multiple investors to invest in a diversified portfolio of ethically selected companies. These funds are specifically designed to align with various social responsibility criteria.

4. *Leverage Resources:* Even from prison, you can access resources that provide information about socially responsible companies and funds. Libraries may have books and magazines on the subject, and many institutions provide access to financial publications. If you have internet access, there are myriad websites dedicated to SRI.

Tips to Evaluate Companies for SRI

- *Environmental Impact:* Look for companies that have strong environmental policies. This includes reducing carbon emissions, using renewable energy, and having recycling programs.
- *Social Practices:* Consider how companies treat their employees and the communities they operate in. Fair wages, good working conditions, and community engagement are key factors.
- *Governance:* Evaluate companies based on their business ethics, transparency, and leadership

practices. Are they honest and straightforward in their dealings?

Resources for Learning More

- *Financial Publications:* Magazines like "Forbes," "Barron's," and "The Economist" often include sections on ethical investing.
- *Investment Guides:* Books specifically about SRI can provide in-depth knowledge and strategies.
- *Educational Programs:* Some prisons offer financial literacy courses where you may learn about SRI.

Final Thoughts

Making socially responsible investment choices is all about aligning your financial goals with your ethical values. It's not just about making money—it's about making a difference. As you start your investing journey from prison, remember that by choosing to invest ethically, you're taking a stand for what you believe in and contributing to the greater good. This can be both a rewarding and fulfilling aspect of your investment strategy.

Mental Health and Emotional Well-being in Investing

"Investing isn't just about numbers; it's about understanding the emotions that guide those numbers."
Unknown

Understanding the Psychological Aspects of Investing

INVESTING IN THE STOCK MARKET IS NOT JUST ABOUT NUMBERS and strategies; it's also about managing your emotions and maintaining your mental health. Incarceration brings difficulties and stresses, which can amplify the psychological aspects of investing. Understanding these can help you make more rational decisions and safeguard your emotional well-being.

. . .

FEAR AND GREED: THE EMOTIONAL PENDULUM

TWO OF THE MOST POWERFUL EMOTIONS IN INVESTING ARE *FEAR* and *greed*. Fear can lead to panic-selling when stock prices drop, while greed might push you to take unnecessary risks hoping for bigger gains. Both can result in significant financial losses if not managed properly. In prison, these emotions can be intensified by feelings of helplessness or urgency.

STRATEGIES TO MANAGE FEAR AND GREED:

- *Stay Informed, Not Overwhelmed:* Rely on your outside assistant to keep you updated on market conditions without flooding you with information. Set boundaries for how often you need updates.
- *Create a Plan and Stick to It:* Develop a comprehensive investment strategy with the help of your assistant and adhere to it. This can act as an anchor during volatile times.
- *Take a Long-Term Perspective:* Remember that investing is a marathon, not a sprint. Short-term fluctuations are normal.

. . .

The Importance of Patience and Discipline

In the stock market, *patience* and *discipline* are your best allies. Most successful investors make their fortunes by holding onto their investments long-term rather than by rapidly trading.

Building Patience and Discipline:

- *Meditation and Mindfulness:* Practicing mindfulness can help you stay calm and focused. Techniques such as deep breathing, meditation, or journaling your thoughts can be invaluable.
- *Routine and Consistency:* Develop a routine for checking in on your investments and stick with it. Consistency helps build discipline.

Emotional Support Systems

. . .

BEING IN PRISON CAN LEAD TO FEELINGS OF ISOLATION THAT can negatively affect your mental health, thus impacting your investment decisions. Having a support system in place can make a big difference.

TYPES OF SUPPORT:

- *Trusted Assistant:* Ensure that your outside assistant is someone you can trust, who understands your goals and can provide not just logistical help but emotional support as well.
- *Peer Groups:* Engage with fellow inmates who have similar investment interests. Sharing your experiences and challenges can reduce the feeling of isolation.
- *Mental Health Resources:* Utilize any available mental health services within the prison. Counseling and therapy can be beneficial for managing stress and anxiety.

DECISION-MAKING UNDER STRESS

. . .

MAKING INVESTMENT DECISIONS WHILE STRESSED CAN LEAD TO mistakes. It's essential to recognize when you're feeling over-whelmed and to take steps to manage that stress before making any financial decisions.

MANAGING STRESS:

- *Break Down Decisions:* Simplify complex decisions into smaller, manageable parts. This can make the decision-making process less of a hassle.
- *Time-Outs:* Give yourself permission to take breaks. Sometimes, stepping away for a moment can provide clarity.
- *Healthy Outlets:* Engage in activities that divert your mind from stress, such as reading, exercising, or creative expression.

UNDERSTANDING THE PSYCHOLOGICAL ASPECTS OF INVESTING IS crucial, especially in a high-stress, confined environment like prison. By managing your emotions, seeking support, and maintaining mental discipline, you can not only become a more successful investor but also ensure your emotional well-being. Keep in mind that the stock market is unpredictable, but with the right psychological tools, you can navigate it more effectively.

Coping with Stress and Emotions Related to Financial Decisions

Investing in the stock market can be a thrilling experience, but it can also come with significant emotional highs and lows. This is especially true when you're investing from prison, where the limitations and constraints of your environment might add an extra layer of stress. *Understanding how to manage these emotions and cope with stress* is critical for making rational and well-informed financial decisions.

I. Understanding Emotional Reactions

Emotions like fear, greed, and anxiety often play significant roles in financial decision-making. Fear might prevent you from taking calculated risks, while greed could push you to make impulsive decisions that lack careful consideration. Anxiety might cause you to second-guess your choices continually, leading to paralysis by analysis. It's essential to acknowledge these feelings instead of ignoring them.

2. The Role of Outside Assistants

SINCE YOUR PHYSICAL LIMITATIONS PREVENT DIRECT ACCESS TO financial markets, you rely on an outside assistant to execute trades and gather information. This adds another complexity: *the fear of delegation.* Trusting someone else with your financial decisions requires you to relinquish some control, which can be stressful. Ensure that you have clear, open communication and a solid understanding with your assistant about your financial goals and strategies to mitigate this stress.

3. Developing a Routine

CREATING A STRUCTURED ROUTINE AROUND YOUR INVESTMENT activities can help mitigate stress. Set specific times for receiving updates from your assistant and reviewing your investment strategy. A routine provides predictability and control, reducing the anxiety that stems from uncertainty.

4. Mindfulness and Stress-Relief Techniques

MINDFULNESS TECHNIQUES SUCH AS DEEP-BREATHING exercises, meditation, and journaling can help clear your mind and reduce stress. Even simple practices, like taking a few minutes each day to focus on your breath or writing down your thoughts and feelings, can make a significant difference in your emotional well-being.

5. Educating Yourself

KNOWLEDGE IS POWER, AND THE MORE INFORMED YOU ARE about how the stock market works, the more confident you will feel in your decision-making. Utilize available prison resources like educational programs, books, and access to financial news (if permissible) to continually expand your investing knowledge. This education can serve as an anchor, grounding you when market fluctuations and external pressures threaten to overwhelm you.

6. Support Systems

DON'T UNDERESTIMATE THE IMPORTANCE OF HAVING A SUPPORT system, even from within prison. Bonds with fellow inmates, family members, or even prison counselors who understand your goals can provide the emotional support needed to navigate the ups and downs of investing. Venting your frustrations and sharing your successes with others can be incredibly therapeutic.

7. Setting Realistic Expectations

IT'S VITAL TO SET REALISTIC EXPECTATIONS FOR YOUR investments. The stock market is inherently volatile, and returns are not guaranteed. Preparing for both favorable and unfavorable outcomes can help you maintain emotional balance and avoid drastic reactions driven by panic or euphoria.

. . .

IN SUMMARY, MANAGING STRESS AND EMOTIONS ASSOCIATED with financial decisions is a multifaceted task that involves understanding your emotional reactions, leveraging outside assistance effectively, developing structured routines, practicing mindfulness, continually educating yourself, building a support system, and setting realistic expectations. By addressing these factors, you can foster a healthier, more resilient mindset that will assist you in making sound investment decisions, even from the confines of prison.

SEEKING SUPPORT AND MAINTAINING A POSITIVE MINDSET

INVESTING IN THE STOCK MARKET CAN BE A ROLLERCOASTER OF emotions, especially when dealing with the unique challenges of being incarcerated. It's crucial to not only focus on your financial goals but also prioritize your mental health and emotional well-being. Keeping a positive mindset and seeking support can make a significant difference in your investing journey.

1. Building a Support Network

. . .

IN THE CONTEXT OF INCARCERATION, HAVING A ROBUST SUPPORT network is imperative. You will require outside assistance for various tasks, and emotional and mental support are no exception. Here's how you can build and utilize a strong support network:

- *Family and Friends:* Reach out to family members and friends who might be willing to assist you with your investment goals. They can provide both emotional support and practical assistance, such as carrying out transactions on your behalf.

- *Pen Pals and Mentorship Programs:* Various organizations offer pen pal and mentorship programs where volunteers communicate with incarcerated individuals. Engaging with someone who has knowledge about investing can be instrumental in providing guidance and moral support.

- *Support Groups:* Many prisons have support groups or clubs where inmates can share experiences and knowledge. If such a group exists in your facility, joining it can offer a sense of community and enable you to learn from others.

2. Education and Self-Improvement

STAYING POSITIVE OFTEN MEANS KEEPING YOURSELF OCCUPIED with constructive activities. Utilize the opportunities available to enhance your knowledge about investing and other relevant skills:

- *Educational Programs:* Many prisons offer educational programs, including courses on financial literacy. Enroll in these programs to build a strong foundation in investing.

- *Reading and Research:* Make good use of any reading material available to you. Apart from books about investing, read newspapers and financial magazines to stay updated on market trends.

3. Emotional Resilience

INVESTING INVOLVES RISKS, AND THE STOCK MARKET CAN BE unpredictable. Here are some strategies to build emotional resilience:

- *Mindfulness and Meditation:* Practicing mindfulness and meditation can help you stay grounded and manage stress. Many prisons offer yoga or meditation sessions; participate in these to build your emotional strength.

- *Positive Affirmations:* Use positive affirmations to reinforce your confidence in your abilities and in your investing decisions. For instance, remind yourself that every step you take is a learning experience.

- *Balanced Perspective:* Understand that losses are part of the investing experience, just as much as gains. Maintaining a balanced perspective can prevent you from becoming overly discouraged by setbacks.

4. **Setting Realistic Goals**

SETTING ACHIEVABLE AND REALISTIC GOALS CAN GIVE YOU A clear direction and help maintain your motivation:

- *Short-term Goals:* Create short-term goals that can provide an immediate sense of accomplishment. For instance, aim to learn one new investing concept each week.

- *Long-term Vision:* Keep a long-term perspective on your investment journey. Understand that building wealth through investing is a gradual process that requires patience and persistence.

IN CLOSING, MAINTAINING A POSITIVE MINDSET AND SEEKING support are essential components of your investing journey from prison. By building a robust support network, continually educating yourself, fostering emotional resilience, and setting realistic goals, you can navigate the complexities of investing with greater confidence and mental well-being. Remember, prioritizing your mental health is not just beneficial for investing but is crucial for your overall well-being and future success

Investment Strategies for Inmates

"You can't predict the market, but you can cultivate a mindset of resilience and adaptability. It's all about how you respond to what life throws your way."
Howard Marks

Exploring Advanced Trading Techniques

Once you have a solid understanding of basic investment principles and have established a cooperative relationship with an outside assistant to help manage your trades, it's time to delve into some advanced trading techniques. These methods can potentially enhance your investing strategy, allowing for higher returns, but they do come with increased risk like the Call and Put Options that we discussed in Chapter 7, which require an in-depth understanding of market movements and implications of derivative products.

So, it's crucial to research and possibly practice with virtual trading platforms before committing real funds. Remember, these trades must be executed by your outside assistant with precise instructions from you.

1. Technical Analysis:

Technical analysis involves studying past market data, primarily price and volume, to forecast future price movements. Here are some basic concepts used in technical analysis:

- *Charts and Patterns:* Historical price charts and patterns, like "head and shoulders" or "double tops and bottoms," are used to predict future movements.

- *Indicators and Oscillators:* Tools like moving averages, Relative Strength Index (RSI), and MACD (Moving Average Convergence Divergence) help analyze and interpret price trends and market momentum.

- *Support and Resistance Levels:* These are specific price points on a chart expected to be key levels of buying or selling interest.

Given the nature of incarceration, you'll rely on your assistant to provide you with the relevant data and execute trades based on your analysis.

2. Margin Trading:

Margin trading involves borrowing money from a brokerage to buy more stock than you could with only your available funds. Here's how it works:

- *Borrowing Funds:* You open a margin account and use it to borrow money from your broker to buy stocks. The stocks purchased serve as collateral for the loan.

- *Leverage:* This borrowing allows you to leverage your investments, potentially increasing both gains and losses.

It's important to exercise caution with margin trading, as it can magnify your profits but also your losses. Make sure your assistant understands and monitors the margin account closely to avoid margin calls (demands by brokers to add funds to the account when the value of the collateral drops).

3. Short Selling:

Short selling is a technique where you sell borrowed stocks, anticipating that the price will drop so you can buy them back at a lower price. Here's a basic rundown:

- *Sell High, Buy Low:* You "borrow" shares from your broker and sell them at the current market price. Then, you hope the stock price falls so you can repurchase the shares at a lower price, return them to the lender, and pocket the difference.

- *Risks:* The risk of short selling lies in the fact that if the stock price rises instead of falls, you might face potentially unlimited losses since you need to repurchase the shares at a higher price.

In the context of incarceration, communicating timely and accurate instructions to your assistant is essential for executing short sales effectively.

Conclusion

Exploring advanced trading techniques like options trading, technical analysis, margin trading, and short selling can significantly enhance your investment strategy. However, these techniques come with increased risk and complexity. Always educate yourself thoroughly and work closely with your outside assistant to ensure these advanced strategies are executed correctly and align with your investment goals. Patience, diligence, and continuous learning are key components to mastering these advanced investment strategies even from within prison.

LEVERAGING FINANCIAL DERIVATIVES FOR HEDGING AND Speculation

IN THIS SECTION, WE'LL TAKE A LOOK AT AN ADVANCED AREA OF investing called financial derivatives. You may have heard the term "derivatives" on finance shows or in the news, usually with some excitement or anxiety. Derivatives can indeed be powerful tools in the hands of skilled investors, whether they are used for hedging to reduce risk or speculation to potentially increase returns. But what exactly are derivatives, and how can you leverage them to your advantage from inside prison? Let's break it down.

UNDERSTANDING FINANCIAL DERIVATIVES

FIRST, LET'S CLARIFY WHAT DERIVATIVES ARE. A *FINANCIAL derivative* is a contract whose value is based on, or "derived" from, the performance of an underlying financial asset, index, or other investment. Common types of derivatives include options, futures, and swaps. Here's a simple way to think about each:

- *Options:* A contract that gives the buyer the right, but not the obligation, to buy or sell an asset at a specific price before a specified date.
- *Futures:* A contract obligating the buyer to purchase, or the seller to sell, an asset at a predetermined future date and price.
- *Swaps:* Agreements between two parties to exchange sequences of cash flows for a set period of time.

Why Use Derivatives?

DERIVATIVES CAN BE USED FOR TWO PRIMARY PURPOSES: hedging and speculation.

1. *Hedging:* This involves using derivatives to reduce the risk of adverse price movements in an asset. For example, if you or your outside assistant has

invested in a particular stock, you could buy options to sell that stock at a set price (called a "put option"), thus ensuring that you can limit your losses if the stock price falls.

2. *Speculation:* This is essentially betting on the future price movement of an asset to potentially earn high returns. For example, you could buy an option to purchase a stock at a set price (called a "call option"), hoping that its price will increase so you can sell at a higher profit.

STEPS TO LEVERAGE DERIVATIVES FROM PRISON

1. *Use Your Outside Assistant:* Since trading derivatives is complex and generally requires a broker, you'll need your outside assistant to handle the actual transactions. Make sure they are educated about derivatives or, preferable, work with a qualified financial advisor.

2. *Research Thoroughly:* Before instructing your assistant, gather as much knowledge as you can about the specific derivative you are interested in. Books, articles, and reliable internet sources are your friends here.

3. *Start Small:* If you're new to derivatives, start with smaller, simpler transactions to minimize risk. For example, you could try buying a single call option instead of diving into futures or swaps.

4. *Set Clear Instructions:* Clearly communicate your strategy and risk tolerance to your outside assistant. For example, you might say, "I want to hedge my investment in XYZ stock by buying put options with a strike price of $50, expiring in three months."

5. *Monitor Regularly:* Stay informed about the performance of your investments and the overall

market conditions. Regularly check in with your assistant to see how your strategy is playing out.

FINAL THOUGHTS

LEVERAGING FINANCIAL DERIVATIVES CAN BE A SOPHISTICATED way to manage investments from prison, but it is crucial to proceed cautiously. These instruments can be quite complex and involve significant risk, especially if you are speculating rather than hedging. Use derivatives as part of a balanced investment strategy and always keep communication open with your outside assistant or advisor to ensure you stay on course. With the right knowledge and tools, even incarcerated investors can participate in advanced financial strategies.

IMPLEMENTING SOPHISTICATED INVESTMENT STRATEGIES through Trusted Contacts

AT THIS POINT IN YOUR INVESTMENT JOURNEY, YOU LIKELY understand the importance of having an outside assistant to help manage certain tasks that you cannot perform from within the confines of a correctional facility. Now, let's delve into how you can implement sophisticated investment strategies through these trusted contacts.

The Role of a Trusted Contact

As stated in Chapter 4, your trusted contact is essentially an extension of your investment strategy. The key is that this person must be reliable, understand your investment goals, and be willing to execute the strategies you develop. Clear communication and mutual understanding are crucial in this partnership.

Educating Your Trusted Contact

Your trusted contact should be well-versed in basic and advanced investment concepts. Consider creating or borrowing simple educational materials, like summaries of key concepts or step-by-step guides on how to perform specific transactions. This way, they'll be equipped to make informed decisions or seek further clarification when necessary.

. . .

Developing a Strategy Together

In order to implement sophisticated strategies, you need a well-thought-out plan that both you and your trusted contact can follow. Here are some steps to get started:

1. Identify Investment Goals:

Clearly outline what you aim to achieve with your investments—whether it's long-term growth, income generation, or a combination of both.

2. Research and Analysis:

Utilize available resources to conduct thorough research on potential stocks or investment opportunities. Your trusted contact can help you by accessing online tools, financial reports, and market news.

3. Diversification:

ONE ADVANCED STRATEGY INVOLVES DIVERSIFYING YOUR portfolio to mitigate risks. Discuss with your trusted contact how to allocate investments across different sectors, industries, or types of assets.

4. Risk Management:

DEVELOP A RISK MANAGEMENT PLAN WHICH INCLUDES SETTING stop-loss orders, diversifying investments, and not putting all your funds into high-risk stocks. Explain to your trusted contact how to monitor and adjust these settings.

5. Regular Monitoring and Adjustment:

FINANCIAL MARKETS ARE DYNAMIC, AND YOUR INVESTMENT strategy should be flexible. Set up regular check-ins with your trusted contact to review the performance of your investments and make necessary adjustments.

Utilizing Advanced Tools and Resources

Many advanced investment strategies require timely data and sophisticated analysis tools. Here's how you and your trusted contact can leverage these:

- **Stock Screeners:**

These are online tools that help filter stocks based on specific criteria. Your contact can use these to identify stocks that meet your investment strategies.

- **Financial News Services:**

Staying updated with financial news is critical. Your trusted contact should regularly check financial news websites, subscribe to newsletters, or use apps that provide market news.

- **Technical Analysis Software:**

FOR MORE ADVANCED STRATEGIES, TECHNICAL ANALYSIS software can help in performing pattern recognition, predictive modeling, and other statistical analyses. If your contact has access to these tools, they can provide you with insightful data to inform your decisions.

IMPLEMENTING ORDERS AND TRANSACTIONS

EXECUTING TRADES EFFECTIVELY IS A PRACTICAL ASPECT OF implementing sophisticated strategies. Your trusted contact should be familiar with:

- **Order Types:**

UNDERSTAND AND KNOW WHEN TO USE DIFFERENT ORDER TYPES like market orders, limit orders, and stop orders.

- **Trading Platforms:**

THEY'LL NEED TO BE PROFICIENT IN USING AN ONLINE brokerage platform to place trades, check balances, and review transaction histories.

- **Fee Structures:**

BE AWARE OF THE FEE STRUCTURES OF THE CHOSEN BROKERAGE and seek to minimize transaction costs.

BUILDING AND MAINTAINING TRUST

LASTLY, *TRANSPARENCY* AND *TRUST* ARE PARAMOUNT IN YOUR relationship with your contact. Consider setting up regular audits where you both review the activities together to ensure everything is proceeding according to plan. This helps in maintaining transparency and keeping your investments on track.

BY LEVERAGING THE SKILLS AND RESOURCES OF A TRUSTED contact, you can execute sophisticated investment strategies, even from within a prison environment. Open communication, mutual understanding, and ongoing education are the keystones that will drive your investment success.

Navigating Market Volatility and Uncertainty

"In this business, if you're good, you're right six times out of ten.
You're never going
to be right nine times out of ten."
Peter Lynch

<u>Strategies for Dealing with Market Fluctuations</u>

WHEN IT COMES TO INVESTING IN THE STOCK MARKET, ONE thing is for certain: the market will go up and down. These ups and downs are known as market fluctuations, and they are a normal part of investing. It's important not to let these fluctuations scare you away from investing altogether. Instead, you can use specific strategies to navigate these changes wisely. Let's break down some effective strategies for dealing with market fluctuations:

1. Diversify Your Investments

Diversification means spreading your investments across different types of stocks and other assets. Think of it like not putting all your eggs in one basket. This way, if one part of the market is doing poorly, other investments may be doing well, balancing things out.

For example:

- Invest in different industries (like technology, healthcare, and utilities).
- Consider different types of assets, such as bonds, mutual funds, or even real estate, through Real Estate Investment Trusts (REITs).

2. Long-Term Perspective

. . .

THE STOCK MARKET CAN BE VERY UNPREDICTABLE IN THE SHORT term, but over the long term, it tends to grow. This means that if you leave your money invested for many years, you are more likely to see positive returns.

HERE'S HOW TO ADOPT A LONG-TERM PERSPECTIVE:

- Make a plan to hold your investments for at least 5 to 10 years.
- Don't panic and sell just because the market has dropped; remember that it may recover and grow over time.
- Think of market drops as "sales" where you can buy stocks at a lower price.

3. CONSISTENT INVESTMENT APPROACH

REGULARLY INVESTING SMALLER AMOUNTS OVER TIME RATHER than making large single investments, helps smooth out market fluctuations. This approach is known as *dollar-cost averaging.*

. . .

HERE'S HOW IT WORKS:

- Set a regular schedule to invest, such as monthly or quarterly.
- Invest the same amount each time, regardless of whether the market is up or down.
- This strategy ensures you buy more shares when prices are low and fewer shares when prices are high.

4. STAY INFORMED, BUT NOT OBSESSED

KEEPING YOURSELF INFORMED ABOUT MARKET TRENDS AND THE performance of your investments is important, but it's equally important not to obsess over every little change.

HERE'S A BALANCED WAY TO STAY INFORMED:

- Set up a system with your assistant to receive regular, but not overwhelming, updates. This could be monthly or quarterly summaries of your investment account.

- Focus on major news and trends that could have long-term impacts rather than daily market noise.

5. SET CLEAR GOALS AND STICK TO THEM

HAVING CLEAR FINANCIAL GOALS CAN HELP YOU STAY FOCUSED and calm during market fluctuations.

HERE'S A STEP-BY-STEP ON GOAL SETTING:

- Define what you're investing for (e.g., a retirement fund, helping family, starting a business when you get out).
- Set specific, achievable targets and a timeline to reach them.
- Review these goals periodically with your assistant but avoid making drastic changes based solely on market conditions.

6. BUILD AN EMERGENCY FUND

EVEN WHILE INVESTING, IT'S CRUCIAL TO HAVE AN EMERGENCY fund. This is a separate stash of money that you can use if you need cash quickly without having to sell your investments at a bad time.

HERE'S HOW TO SET ONE UP:

- Aim to save about 3 to 6 months' worth of living expenses in a liquid account, like a savings account.
- This financial cushion helps you ride out market downturns without needing to cash out your investments.

7. UNDERSTAND RISK TOLERANCE

EVERYONE HAS A DIFFERENT LEVEL OF COMFORT WITH TAKING risks, known as risk tolerance.

. . .

REFLECT ON YOUR OWN RISK TOLERANCE:

- Acknowledge how much market fluctuation you're comfortable with.
- Choose investments that align with your level of risk tolerance. Higher-risk investments usually offer higher potential returns but also come with more volatility.

BY EMPLOYING THESE STRATEGIES, YOU CAN NAVIGATE MARKET fluctuations with more confidence and less stress. Remember, market ups and downs are just part of the journey, and having a steady, informed approach will help keep you on the path to achieving your investment goals.

LONG-TERM PERSPECTIVE IN VOLATILE MARKET CONDITIONS

INVESTING IN THE STOCK MARKET CAN FEEL LIKE RIDING A rollercoaster, especially during times of volatility and uncertainty. Prices can swing wildly due to economic news, political events, or even unexpected global crises. For aspiring investors, especially those navigating from within the constraints of prison, these fluctuations can be intimidating. However, understanding market volatility and embracing a long-term perspective can make a significant difference in your investment journey.

What is Market Volatility?

MARKET VOLATILITY REFERS TO THE DEGREE OF VARIATION IN the price of a stock or the stock market as a whole over a given period. High volatility means prices move up and down rapidly in short time frames, while low volatility indicates more stable prices. It's like the difference between sailing in choppy waters and smooth seas.

VOLATILITY IS OFTEN DRIVEN BY NEWS, INVESTOR EMOTIONS, and major economic changes. Even the rumor of a company's downturn can cause its stock price to fluctuate. While these movements can seem scary, they also present opportunities for savvy investors.

Why a Long-term Perspective Matters

1. *Historically Higher Returns:* Despite short-term ups and downs, the stock market has consistently delivered positive returns over the long-term. By holding your investments for several years, you can ride out the downturns and benefit from the overall upward trend.

2. *Reduction of Risk:* Long-term investing helps mitigate the risks associated with market volatility. The longer your investment horizon, the lower the impact of short-term market fluctuations on your overall returns.

3. *Compounding:* Time allows your investments to grow exponentially through the power of compounding. Reinvesting dividends and interests (when allowed and facilitated by your outside assistant) can lead to significantly higher returns over time.

STRATEGIES FOR NAVIGATING VOLATILE MARKETS

1. *Diversification:* Spread your investments across different sectors, industries, and asset classes. Diversification reduces the impact of a poor-performing stock or sector on your overall portfolio. Consult with your outside assistant to help choose a mix of investments that align with your risk tolerance and goals.

2. *Dollar-Cost Averaging:* This involves consistently investing a fixed amount of money at regular intervals, regardless of market conditions. This strategy can help lower the average cost of the investments over time and reduce the impact of market volatility.

3. *Stay Informed but Avoid Overreacting:* Keep yourself informed about market trends and news. However, avoid making impulsive decisions based on short-term news. Remember, not all market

news requires action. Discuss significant market developments with your outside assistant to get a balanced understanding before making any decisions.

4. *Focus on Quality Investments:* Invest in companies with strong fundamentals, including robust financial health, a solid track record, and competent management. High-quality stocks are more likely to recover from market downturns.

EMOTIONAL DISCIPLINE

MARKET VOLATILITY CAN TRIGGER FEAR AND ANXIETY. IT'S crucial to maintain emotional discipline and stick to your long-term investment plan. Here are some tips:

- *Set Realistic Goals:* Have clear, realistic investment goals. Understand that achieving considerable gains takes time.

- *Avoid Frequent Monitoring:* Constantly checking stock prices can heighten anxiety. Instead, review your portfolio periodically.
- *Seek Support:* Utilize your outside assistant not only for logistical support but also for emotional encouragement. They can provide a rational perspective during tumultuous times.

LEVERAGING EXTERNAL SUPPORT

AS AN INCARCERATED INVESTOR, YOU'VE ALREADY UNDERSTOOD the importance of having an outside assistant. They can help with tasks such as:

- Executing trades on your behalf.
- Keeping abreast of market news and updates.
- Facilitating the reinvestment of dividends.
- Providing regular portfolio updates.

ALWAYS MAINTAIN CLEAR, ONGOING COMMUNICATION WITH

your assistant to ensure your long-term strategy is consistently applied, even during volatile periods.

ULTIMATELY, NAVIGATING MARKET VOLATILITY REQUIRES A blend of knowledge, strategy, and emotional resilience. By adopting a long-term perspective and leveraging the support of your outside assistant, you can turn market fluctuations into opportunities for growth. *Patience* and *discipline* are your allies in the journey towards successful investing, even from within the confines of prison.

MAINTAINING DISCIPLINE AND STAYING FOCUSED ON Investment Goals

INVESTING IN THE STOCK MARKET OFTEN INVOLVES NAVIGATING through periods of volatility and uncertainty. These times can be challenging even for seasoned investors, but they are especially daunting for beginners. As an incarcerated aspiring investor, maintaining discipline and staying focused on your investment goals becomes even more crucial. Let's break down how you can achieve this, despite the unique constraints you face.

. . .

UNDERSTANDING MARKET VOLATILITY

MARKET VOLATILITY REFERS TO SIGNIFICANT UPWARD AND downward movements in the price of stocks. These fluctuations can occur due to a variety of reasons, including economic events, changes in market sentiment, political events, and global crises. It's important to understand that:

1. *Volatility is Normal:* The stock market is naturally volatile. Prices go up and down regularly, and this is part of the normal market cycle.
2. *Short-Term vs. Long-Term:* Volatility has more impact in the short term. Over longer periods, markets have historically trended upwards, despite short-term noise.

SETTING CLEAR INVESTMENT GOALS

BEFORE YOU START INVESTING, IT'S CRUCIAL TO SET CLEAR, achievable goals. This will give you a roadmap to follow, helping you stay focused even when the market is turbulent. Your goals might include:

. . .

1. *Wealth Accumulation:* Growing your investment portfolio over time to build wealth.
2. *Income Generation:* Creating a stream of income from dividends or interest.
3. *Capital Preservation:* Ensuring that your initial investment amount doesn't decrease significantly.

ONCE YOUR GOALS ARE SET, IT'S EASIER TO MAKE DECISIONS that align with them.

MAINTAINING DISCIPLINE

MAINTAINING DISCIPLINE IN INVESTING MEANS STICKING TO your plan and not making impulsive decisions based on short-term market movements. Here's how you can maintain discipline:

1. *Stick to Your Plan:* Trust the investment plan you've created. If your research indicates that your

investments are solid, hold onto them rather than selling in a panic.

2. *Avoid Emotional Investing:* Emotions like fear and greed can lead to poor investment decisions. Work with your outside assistant to stay objective.

3. *Regular Reviews:* Periodically review your investment portfolio with your assistant to ensure it aligns with your goals and make necessary adjustments.

STAYING FOCUSED DURING UNCERTAINTY

MARKET UNCERTAINTY IS INEVITABLE. HERE'S HOW YOU CAN stay focused on your investment goals during these times:

1. *Diversification:* Spread your investments across different asset classes (stocks, bonds, etc.) and sectors to reduce risk. A diversified portfolio can better withstand market turbulence.

2. *Long-Term Perspective:* Stay focused on the long-term potential of your investments rather than getting caught up in daily market fluctuations.

3. *Education:* Continue educating yourself about investing. The more you understand what drives market movements, the easier it will be to stay calm and make informed decisions.

LEVERAGING YOUR OUTSIDE ASSISTANT

SINCE YOU'LL NEED HELP EXECUTING CERTAIN TASKS, USE YOUR outside assistant effectively:

1. *Clear Communication:* Ensure you clearly communicate your investment goals and plans with your assistant.
2. *Regular Updates:* Ask your assistant to provide regular updates on market conditions and your portfolio's performance.
3. *Guidance and Support:* Seek their guidance on major decisions, but always make sure it aligns with your long-term goals.

BY MAINTAINING DISCIPLINE AND FOCUSING ON YOUR LONG-term investment goals, you can navigate market volatility and uncertainty more effectively. This approach will help you build a robust portfolio, even from the constraints of prison, and set you on a path toward financial growth and stability.

Empowering Others Through Financial Education

*"Imagine a world where financial literacy is a common skill; we can make that
a reality through consistent education and support."*
Troy Milings

Sharing investment knowledge with fellow inmates

One of the most impactful ways you can solidify your own understanding of the stock market and empower others at the same time is by sharing what you've learned with your fellow inmates. Building a small community around financial education not only creates a supportive learning environment but also helps in refining your knowledge through collective discussions and problem-solving. Here's how you can make that happen:

Start Informal Study Groups

Organize informal study groups where you can discuss basic investing concepts such as stocks, bonds, mutual funds, and index funds. Use the knowledge you've gained so far to break down these concepts into easily digestible bits. For example, explain stocks as partial ownership in a company, and mutual funds as pooled investments managed by professionals.

Use Analogies and Simple Language

Technical jargon can be overwhelming for beginners. Simplify complex investment terms by using relatable analogies. For instance, describe a stock as a slice of pizza; owning all the slices means you own the whole pizza (the company), but owning just one slice means you share ownership with others. Using simple language makes the concepts more approachable and less intimidating.

Share Resources

Books, pamphlets, or printed articles can serve as valuable resources. If you have access to these through your outside assistant, make sure to circulate them among your peers. Utilize the prison library if it has finance-related books and create a list of recommended readings for your study group.

Role-playing and Simulation

Create simulations or role-playing exercises to make learning interactive. For example, simulate a stock market scenario where each member picks a stock, tracks its performance over time, and discusses why its value might have gone up or down. This hands-on approach can make abstract concepts more concrete and understandable.

Encourage Questions and Discussions

Foster an environment where everyone feels comfortable asking questions. No question is too basic. By addressing questions and doubts, everyone, including yourself, can deepen their understanding. Encourage discussions and debates where group members can share different perspectives and insights.

Guest Speakers via Calls

Coordinate with your outside assistant to arrange calls or video conferences with financial experts. These sessions can offer invaluable insights and answer more advanced questions. Make sure to prepare in advance and submit questions to the expert through your assistant to make the most out of these sessions.

Create Financial Goals

Teach and encourage others to set realistic financial goals. Whether it's saving a small amount from their commissary or understanding how to invest once they are on the outside, having clear financial goals can provide direction and motivation.

Accountability and Progress Tracking

Set up a system to track your progress and that of your peers. Regularly reviewing this progress keeps everyone accountable and motivated. Celebrate small wins, such as successfully understanding a new concept or making a mock "investment" that yields a positive return.

By taking these steps, you can not only solidify your own investment knowledge but also create a supportive community that empowers everyone involved. Sharing investment knowledge isn't just about teaching others; it's about building a network of mutual growth and self-improvement.

Mentoring Others in Financial Literacy and Investing

Mentoring plays a crucial role in fostering financial literacy and investing skills among incarcerated individuals. If you've gained some knowledge about investing in the stock market, passing that information on can be empowering for both you and your peers. Here is a step-by-step guide to mentoring others in financial literacy and investing:

1. **Start with the Basics:**

   - Before diving into specific investment strategies, ensure your mentees understand fundamental concepts like saving, budgeting, and the value of money over time. Use simple language and relate these concepts to everyday experiences within the prison environment.

3. **Explain Key Financial Terms:**

- Introduce terms such as assets, liabilities, stocks, bonds, dividends, and capital gains. Create a glossary of financial terms to refer back to and use examples to make these abstract concepts more concrete. For instance, you might compare stocks to shares in a business run from a cell: owning more shares means having more influence in business decisions.

4. **Highlight the Importance of Research:**

- Stress the significance of research before making any investment decisions. Teach them how to read financial statements and understand market trends. If possible, share investment resources like financial magazines, newspapers, books available in the prison library, or refer them to purchase this book. Of course, they could read yours, but what if they're shipped off or go to the hole? You could lose your copy depending on how it plays out, or due to the situation, they may have to give it back. That puts them right back at square one, which is bad because this is a book that must be studied and referenced. Either way, it's always good to have your own no matter what it is. In all aspects of life, ownership is key.

4. Demonstrate How to Utilize Outside Assistance:

- Incarcerated individuals often need to rely on someone outside the facility to execute trades and manage investment accounts. Demonstrate how to establish a trustworthy relationship with an outside assistant, such as a family member or friend. Explain the process of communicating investment decisions clearly and keeping detailed records of all transactions.

6. Set Realistic Goals:

- Talk about the importance of setting attainable financial goals, both short-term and long-term. Help your mentees create a simple investment plan tailored to their individual financial situations. Discuss different investment strategies, like long-term holding versus short-term trading, and the risks associated with each.

6. Understand Legal Constraints and Opportunities:

- Ensure everyone is aware of the legal limitations and regulations regarding financial transactions from prison. Discuss any authorized programs or initiatives provided by the prison system that support financial education and literacy.

7. **Encourage Collaborative Learning:**

- Foster a study group environment where peers can share information, ask questions, and support each other. This collaborative approach not only aids in understanding complex topics but also builds a sense of community and shared purpose.

8. **Be Patient and Provide Continuous Support:**

- Financial education can be overwhelming at first. Encourage patience and be prepared to repeat information or explore alternative methods of explanation. Offer continuous support, celebrating their progress and understanding.

9. **Utilize Practical Exercises:**

- Incorporate practical exercises such as mock investment portfolios or budgeting scenarios to apply theoretical knowledge. Role-playing different investment decisions can also provide hands-on experience without the financial risk.

10. Stay Updated and Adapt:

- The financial world is always changing. Stay updated with the latest market trends and share this information with your mentees. Adapt your mentoring techniques based on their evolving needs and the dynamic nature of investment opportunities.

Remember, mentoring is not just about sharing what you know but also inspiring confidence and independence in others. By empowering your peers with financial literacy and investing knowledge, you're helping to build a foundation for their financial future, both in and out of prison.

Building a Community of Informed and Empowered Investors Behind Bars

One of the most powerful aspects of financial education within the prison system is the potential to build a community of informed and empowered investors. By fostering a collaborative environment, you can leverage collective knowledge and support to overcome the unique challenges faced by incarcerated individuals. Here's how you can help build and sustain this community:

1. Share Knowledge and Resources:

Start by sharing what you've learned. Organize informal study groups or discussion circles to talk about investing basics, strategies, and news. Make use of any available educational resources like books, magazines, and newspapers. If anyone in your community has video-based courses or classes on financial topics, these can also be invaluable.

2. Establish a Support Network:

A support network is integral to dealing with the complexities of investing. Designate roles within your community: someone could be responsible for keeping track of financial news, another for researching investment strategies, and others for recording group discussions and insights. This cooperative effort can help distribute the workload and ensure everyone benefits from the collective knowledge.

3. Engage Outside Assistance:

While a lot can be done within the prison walls, there are certain tasks that require outside assistance. For those tasks, like actually executing trades or accessing certain up-to-date financial reports, establish strong communication channels with trusted family members, friends, or legal advisors who can act on your behalf. Regularly updating them with precise and informed instructions is key to this collaboration.

4. Utilize Available Educational Programs:

Many prisons offer educational programs that cover financial management and basic investing. Enroll in these if available. External organizations sometimes partner with prisons to provide courses on financial literacy. Check with your facility to see what programs they offer and how you can take part.

5. Encourage Continuous Learning:

The financial world is constantly evolving, with new trends, regulations, and opportunities emerging. Promote a culture of continuous learning within the community. Stay curious and encourage others to do the same. Use shared learning sessions to stay updated on current events and market movements.

6. Practice and Patience:

Practical application is just as important as theoretical knowledge. Establish mock portfolios and simulate trading scenarios to practice your trading strategies. This will help refine your decision-making process and boost confidence without the risk of actual financial loss.

7. Legal Considerations:

Always be aware of the legal constraints and ethical considerations related to investing from prison. Ensure that everything you do complies with the law and the rules of your facility. Seek guidance from legal advisors or trusted external partners if you are unsure.

8. Inspire and Be Inspired:

As you progress in your financial education, you will likely face obstacles. Sharing stories of success, strategies that worked, and lessons learned from mistakes can be incredibly motivating for others. Your journey can inspire fellow inmates to begin or deepen their financial education, building a robust and dynamic community.

Creating a network of knowledgeable investors requires

effort, dedication, and mutual support. By building a community of informed and empowered investors behind bars, you're not just improving individual prospects but laying the groundwork for widespread financial literacy and empowerment within the prison system.

** UAD **

Thank you for taking the time to read my guide and I hope that it helps you tremendously as you enter the world of investing. Make sure you check out the additional sections and the glossary at the end for more helpful information. Also, if there is a topic that you believe needs to be touched on in my official *How To-From Prison* series, reach out to me and let me know. Don't be surprised if you see your suggestions in the back of an *URBAN AINT DEAD* novel under the coming soon section in the future.

Last but not least, if you support us and what we do, request *URBAN AINT DEAD* titles from your people, local bookstores and prison book distributors. Tell another reader about us and have them do the same. Whether they want Urban Fiction, Black & African American Romance, Urban Erotica, Street Lit or Self-Help for prisoners, we got them covered. Have your trusted contact get this book so they can read it and use it as a reference. Yall may not always be able to talk on the phone, but as long as they have this book, you can make sure yall are on the same page mentally.

Thanks in advance and be on the lookout for *How To Build Your Credit From Prison*.

ABOUT THE AUTHOR

Elijah R. Freeman is an author from Riverdale, Georgia, and a three-time UBAWA Top 100 Author's award winner. Having penned 11 novels so far, he is quickly becoming known as "The Future of Urban Fiction". He is the C.E.O. of URBAN AINT DEAD and has made some of the biggest moves from behind the wall. His books have appeared in KITE Magazine, States Vs. Us, Prison Legal News and Aspiring Authors Magazine.

LEGAL HUSTLES YOU CAN DO FROM PRISONS

Now that you've reached the end of this book it's time to grind, you can't put anything into the market with no money. So how do you legitimately make money in prison? Simple. Use your head. There's all kinds of ways to make money behind the wall, and the surprising thing is, the majority of hustles in prison are *positive*. I've seen my fellow inmates carve bars of soap into beautiful sculptures or draw portraits and then sell them to their neighbors. Others wash clothes, sew, repair electronics, mend damaged shoes, run sports pools, do legal work, operate stores, and cook meals for various people in the dorm for a small fee. Some polish stones they find on the yard and make them into necklaces or furniture; some draw birthday cards; and some sell home-made candy.

Tattoos are always in demand. If you can fashion a tattoo gun from a pen barrel, a few wires, and a sharpened sewing needle— and can draw a reasonably straight line on a fellow inmate's skin — then you'll never want for anything in prison. Some guys even tattoo inmates' plastic cups, engraving names or sports logos for a few dollars' worth of food or hygiene items.

Brewing alcohol is another popular hustle. It's easy enough to smuggle apples out of the chow hall, smash them up in a trash bag, mix in a little sugar, and let it ferment for three or five days. Your homemade alcohol, "Buck," will taste like urine and leave you with a killer hangover, but it will get the job done. And good Buck can make you a few hundred every trip. Buck can also be boiled and distilled in a hot pot to make a cheap form of whiskey called "White Lightning." Highly potent and bitingly sour, White Lightning can go for $50 a bottle where I'm currently at, depending on the quality. But every prison has its own market. Y'all know how that go. If no one's doing it where you are now, congratulations, you control the market!!

Writing was, and still is, my legal hustle behind the wall. If you want to make money writing, have your trusted outside contact visit our website (www.urbanaintdead.com) and submit your manuscript following our submission guide-lines. We offer traditional contracts, but not all manuscripts will be accepted so come with you're A-Game. If your manuscript isn't accepted for a traditional contract, or if you simply don't want to be signed to U.A.D, and would rather do your own thing and have your own company name on your covers, you can hire us to get the job done for you with the same quality and within the same time frame.

Here's a **clean and structured list of services, pricing, and descriptions** for our Assisted Publishing Package Services.

Categories and Services

1. Editing Services

- **Proofreading:** $100
- **Manuscript Editing:**
  - 0-60k words: $350
  - *Contact for a quote for manuscripts over 60k words.*

2. Manuscript Preparation

- **Formatting/Typesetting:** We will prepare and arrange your book's text and interior for printing.
  - **Price:** $100

3. Design Services

- **Cover Design:** $100 (2 free revisions, any additional revisions will be an additional cost)
- **Promo Flyer:** $25
- **Custom Flyer:** *Contact for quote*

4. Distribution Services

- **Amazon KDP Setup:** $25
- **Amazon Upload:** $25 (if you already have an account but just need us to upload it for you)

5. Other Services

- **Typing:** $300 for manuscripts up to 40k words (*Contact for quote for longer projects*).
- **Copyright Registration:** $100 + site registration fees.

Bundled Packages Deals

Bronze Package

- **Includes:**
  - Cover Design
  - Editing
  - Formatting/Typesetting
  - Publishing Consultation

- **Price:** $400

Silver Package

- **Includes:**
  - Cover Design
  - Typing
  - Editing
  - One Flyer
  - Formatting/Typesetting
  - Publishing Consultation
- **Price:** $725

Gold Package

- **Includes:**
  - Cover Design
  - Typing
  - Editing
  - Proofreading
  - Two Flyers
  - Formatting/Typesetting
  - Copyright Registration
  - Publishing Consultation
  - Amazon Upload
- **Price:** $975

Platinum Package

- **Includes:**
  - All-in-One Bundle: Typing, Editing, Proofreading, Formatting/Typesetting
  - Cover Design
  - Three Flyers
  - Publishing Consultation
  - Copyright Registration
  - Amazon Setup & Upload
  - One Month Promotion
  - Amazon Setup/ Upload
- **Price:** $1,200

Once your book is released, you can hire us to promote it to U.A.D's target audience and to whatever audience your book is intended for. Our marketing team now offers three different promotion plans that work with all budgets to increase your book's visibility and help you gain traction.

Tier 1: The Basics Package
    Price: $99
    Target Audience: First-time or budget-conscious authors seeking minimal exposure.
    Perks:

- **Social Media Shoutout:** 3 IG Story posts a week for a month.
- **Inclusion in Newsletter:** Mention in the "Sponsored Showcase" section with a link to the book.
- **Digital Promo Graphic:** A simple branded image featuring the book cover for the author's use (i.e, Available Now flyer)
- **Support Sunday Link In U.A.D FB Group:** Book cover and link in Support Sunday post in group (x4)

Tier 2: The Spotlight Package

Price: $199

Target Audience: Authors looking for a bit more visibility for their release.

Perks:

- **Social Media Shoutout:** 3 IG Story posts a week for a month.
- **Inclusion in Newsletter:** Mention in the "Sponsored Showcase" section with a link to the book.
- **Digital Promo Graphic:** A simple branded image featuring the book cover for the author's use (i.e, Available Now flyer)

- **Support Sunday Link In U.A.D FB Group:** Book cover and link in Support Sunday post in group (x4)
- **FB Group Promo:** Book posted Monday-Friday in over 20 Urban Reader FB Groups for a month.

Tier 3: Maximum Visibility Package

Price: $299

Target Audience: Authors seeking a stronger but still light promotional push.

Perks:

- **Social Media Shoutout:** 3 IG Story posts a week for a month.
- **Inclusion in Newsletter:** Mention in the "Sponsored Showcase" section with a link to the book.
- **Digital Promo Graphic:** A simple branded image featuring the book cover for the author's use (i.e, Available Now flyer)
- **Custom Quote Graphic:** 3 Eye Catching Quote Graphics that can be used on Social Media.
- **3 To 5 Character Visuals:** Visuals of the characters in your book that can be used for promo.
- **Support Sunday Link In U.A.D FB Group:** Book

cover and link in Support Sunday post in group (x4)

- **FB Group Promo:** Book posted Monday-Friday in over 20 Urban Reader FB Groups for a month.
- **Paid Ad:** We will run an Ad for your book for a month on a Sponsored Showcase page with a customized caption, targeting your book's audience to grow your readership.

Whatever you decide to do to come up with the capital needed to invest, move with hast to get it done. There is no time to be stagnant. Build. Stack or starve. If you ever needed a goal to take your mind off of doing time, this is it. Focus on mastering this, then do it. Master the market, and free yourself and your family from the matrix. It's not just about you. This is your gift to them, and everyone else who stayed down.

25 STOCK MARKET BOOKS TO READ THAT

WILL CHANGE YOUR LIFE

1. *The Intelligent Investor* by Benjamin Graham
2. *Security Analysis* by Benjamin Graham and David L. Dodd
3. *Common Stocks and Uncommon Profits* by Philip Fisher
4. *One Up on Wall Street* by Peter Lynch
5. *The Little Book That Still Beats the Market* by Joel Greenblatt
6. *Technical Analysis of the Financial Markets* by John Murphy
7. *A Random Walk Down Wall Street* by Burton Malkiel
8. *Market Wizards* by Jack D. Schwager
9. *Japanese Candlestick Charting Techniques* by Steve Nison

10. *The Essays of Warren Buffett* by Warren Buffett
11. *Reminiscences of a Stock Operator* by Edwin Lefèvre
12. *Beating the Street* by Peter Lynch
13. *The Little Book of Common Sense Investing* by John C. Bogle
14. *Stocks for the Long Run* by Jeremy Siegel
15. *Trade Your Way to Financial Freedom* by Van K. Tharp
16. *Against the Gods: The Remarkable Story of Risk* by Peter L. Bernstein
17. *The Four Pillars of Investing* by William Bernstein
18. *Fooled by Randomness* by Nassim Nicholas Taleb
19. *Manias, Panics, and Crashes: A History of Financial Crises* by Charles P. Kindleberger
20. *The Alchemy of Finance* by George Soros
21. *Barbarians at the Gate* by Bryan Burrough and John Helyar
22. *Flash Boys* by Michael Lewis
23. *The Big Short* by Michael Lewis
24. *When Genius Failed: The Rise and Fall of Long-Term Capital Management* by Roger Lowenstein
25. *Extraordinary Popular Delusions and the Madness of Crowds* by Charles Mackay

"The more that you read, the more things you will know. The more that you learn, the more places you'll go." The famous quote by Dr. Seuss is a short insight into how books can help

you develop the knowledge and power you need to navigate the complexities of the financial market. The books mentioned above act as trusted companions, offering guidance on understanding market dynamics, analyzing company financials, and identifying opportunities for growth and profit.

10 RICHEST INVESTORS IN THE WORLD

1. Warren Buffet – 128.7 Billion
2. Michael Bloomberg – 96.3 Billion
3. Ken Griffen – 37.2 Billion
4. Stephen Schwarzman – 36.8 Billion
5. Jim Simmons – 30.7 Billion
6. Thomas Peterffy – 29.4 Billion
7. Jeff Yass – 28.9 Billion
8. Abigail Johnson – 29.3 Billion
9. R. Budi Hartono – 25.8 Billion
10. Daniel Gilbert – 24.8 Billion

GLOSSARY

A

After-Hours Trading: The buying and selling of securities after the normal trading hours of the stock exchanges.

Alpha: A measure of an investment's performance relative to a benchmark index.

Annual Report: A comprehensive report on a company's activities and financial performance throughout the preceding year.

Arbitrage: The simultaneous purchase and sale of the same asset in different markets to profit from price differences.

Ask Price: The lowest price a seller is willing to accept for a stock.

Asset: Any resource owned by an individual or organization that has economic value.

Average True Range (ATR): A technical analysis indicator that measures market volatility by decomposing the entire range of an asset price for that period.

B

Balance Sheet: A financial statement that summarizes a company's assets, liabilities, and shareholders' equity.

Bear Market: A market condition where prices are falling or are expected to fall.

Beta: A measure of a stock's volatility relative to the overall market.

Bid Price: The highest price a buyer is willing to pay for a stock.

Blue Chip Stocks: Stocks of large, reputable, and financially sound companies with a long history of reliable performance.

Bond: A fixed-income instrument that represents a loan made by an investor to a borrower.

Book Value: The net value of a company's assets found on its balance sheet, calculated as total assets minus intangible assets (patents, goodwill) and liabilities.

Brokerage: A firm or company that buys and sells securities on behalf of investors. Brokerages act as intermediaries between buyers and sellers and charge a fee or commission for their services. There are full-service brokerages, which provide a wide range of services, and discount brokerages, which offer fewer services at lower costs.

Bull Market: A market condition where prices are rising or are expected to rise.

Buyback: When a company buys its own outstanding shares to reduce the number of shares available on the open market, often to increase the value of remaining shares.

C

Call Option: A financial contract that gives the holder the right, but not the obligation, to buy a stock at a specified price within a specific time period.

Candlestick Chart: A type of financial chart that represents the price movements of securities, with each 'candlestick' representing a specific period.

Capital Gain: The profit made from selling a security at a higher price than it was bought.

Capital Loss: The loss made from selling a security at a lower price than it was bought.

Circuit Breaker: A temporary measure used by stock exchanges to curb panic-selling by halting trading for a certain period when price declines reach certain thresholds.

Commission: The fee charged by a broker for executing a trade.

Commodities: Basic goods used in commerce that are interchangeable with other goods of the same type.

Compound Interest: The interest calculated on the initial principal, which also includes all of the accumulated interest from previous periods on a deposit or loan. Compound interest can make a significant difference in the growth of an investment or the cost of a loan over time, as it leads to exponential growth.

Current Ratio: A liquidity ratio that measures a company's ability to pay short-term obligations.

D

Dark Pool: A private financial forum or exchange for trading securities, allowing traders to place large orders without publicly revealing their intentions.

Day Trading: The buying and selling of securities within the same trading day.

Dilution: The reduction in existing shareholders' ownership percentage of a company due to the issuance of additional shares. This typically occurs when a company issues new equity, whether through public offerings, employee stock options, or convertible securities. Dilution can result in a decrease in earnings per share (EPS) and voting power of existing shareholders.

Diversification: Investment strategy involving spreading investments across various sectors or asset classes to minimize risk.

Dividend: A portion of a company's earnings distributed to shareholders.

Dividend Aristocrat: Companies that are part of the S&P 500 index and have increased their dividend payouts for at least 25 consecutive years. While not as prestigious as Dividend Kings, Dividend Aristocrats are still highly regarded for their dividend consistency and financial stability.

Dividend King: A designation for stocks of companies that have consistently increased their dividend payouts to shareholders for at least 50 consecutive years. These companies are typically well-established, financially stable, and often industry leaders. Investing in Dividend Kings can be an attractive strategy for those seeking reliable income through dividends, as well as potential capital appreciation due to the stability and longevity of these companies. These stocks are highly regarded for their ability to sustain and grow dividends through various economic cycles, making them appealing to long-term, income-focused investors.

Dividend Yield: A financial ratio that shows how much a company pays out in dividends relative to its stock price.

Dow Jones Industrial Average (DJIA): A stock index representing 30 significant publicly traded companies in the U.S.

E

Earnings Call: A conference call between the management of a public company, analysts, investors, and the media to discuss the company's financial performance during a specific reporting period, typically quarterly. During the call, management discusses results, future outlook, and answers questions from analysts.

Earnings Per Share (EPS): A company's profit divided by the number of its outstanding shares.

Earnings Report: A financial statement that shows a company's profitability over a specific period.

Employee Stock Options (ESO): A benefit given to employees offering them the option to buy company stock at a discounted price.

Equity: The value of an owner's interest in an asset after deducting liabilities.

Exchange-Traded Fund (ETF): A security that tracks an index, commodity, or basket of assets and trades on an exchange like a stock.

Ex-Dividend Date: The date on which a stock starts trading without the value of its next dividend payment. Investors who purchase the stock on or after this date are not entitled to the dividend.

F

Fibonacci Retracement: A method of technical analysis for determining support and resistance levels based on key numbers identified by the Fibonacci sequence.

Float: The number of shares available for trading by the public.

Forward P/E: The price-to-earnings ratio calculated using forecasted earnings for the next 12 months.

Fundamental Analysis: A method of evaluating securities by analyzing financial data of companies and economic factors.

Futures Contract: A legal agreement to buy or sell a particular commodity or financial instrument at a predetermined price at a specified time in the future.

G

Gamma: The rate of change in an option's delta per one-point move in the underlying asset's price.

Golden Cross: A bullish signal in which a short-term moving average crosses above a long-term moving average.

Greenfield Investment: A type of foreign direct investment where a parent company builds operations in a foreign country from the ground up.

Growth Stocks: Stocks of companies expected to grow their revenues and earnings faster than the market average.

H

Haircut: The difference between the market value of an asset and the value assessed by the lending side of a transaction, used to evaluate risk.

Head and Shoulders: A technical analysis pattern that predicts a bullish-to-bearish trend reversal.

Hedge: An investment made to reduce the risk of adverse price movements in an asset.

High-Frequency Trading (HFT): A type of algorithmic trading characterized by high speeds, high turnover rates, and high order-to-trade ratios.

I

Income Statement: A financial statement that shows a company's revenues and expenses during a particular period.

Index: A statistical measure of the changes in a portfolio of stocks representing a portion of the overall market.

Initial Public Offering (IPO): The first time a company offers shares of its stock to the public.

Insider: An individual who has access to non-public, material information about a company.

Insider Ownership: The percentage of shares that are owned by individuals with access to non-public, material information about the company.

Insider Trading: The buying or selling of stocks based on non-public, material information.

Interest: The cost of borrowing money or the return earned on an investment. Interest can be expressed as a percentage of the principal amount and is typically paid at regular intervals, such as monthly or annually. In the context of loans and borrowing, interest is the fee charged by lenders to borrowers. In the context of investments, interest is the compensation to investors for allowing their money to be used by others.

J.

January Effect: A seasonal increase in stock prices during the month of January, often attributed to increased buying following a year-end tax-loss selling.

Joint Venture (JV): A business arrangement in which two or more parties agree to pool their resources for a specific task.

Junk Bond: A high-yield, high-risk security, typically issued by a company seeking to raise capital quickly in order to finance a takeover.

K

K-1 Form: A tax document used to report the income, losses, and dividends of a partnership.

Keltner Channel: A volatility-based technical analysis indicator composed of three separate lines, similar to Bollinger Bands.

Kiting: The illegal practice of writing a check for which there is not sufficient balance in the account and depositing it in another account in order to cover checks written against that account.

L

Leveraged Buyout (LBO): The acquisition of a company using a significant amount of borrowed money.

Level 2 Quotes: Detailed trading information that provides the bid and ask prices for a security, along with the number of shares available at each price level.

Liability - a financial obligation or debt that an individual or organization owes to another party, requiring future payment.

Limit Order: An order to buy or sell a stock at a specific price or better.

Liquidity: The ability to buy or sell an asset quickly without affecting its price.

Liquidity Ratio: A financial metric used to determine a company's ability to pay off its short-term debts obligations.

M

Margin: Borrowed money that is used to purchase securities.

Market Capitalization (Market Cap): The total market value of a company's outstanding shares.

Market Depth: The market's ability to sustain relatively large market orders without impacting the price of the security.

Moat: A term popularized by Warren Buffett that describes a company's competitive advantage. A moat can come from various sources such as proprietary technology, brand identity, cost advantages, network effects, or high customer loyalty. Companies with wide moats are believed to be able to sustain and grow profits over a long period due to their defensible market position.

Moving Average (MA): A statistical calculation used to analyze data points by creating a series of averages of different subsets of the full data set.

Mutual Fund: An investment vehicle made up of a pool of funds collected from many investors to invest in securities such as stocks, bonds, and other assets.

N

NASDAQ: An American stock exchange, the second-largest in the world by market capitalization.

Net Asset Value (NAV): The value per share of a mutual fund or an ETF.

Net Income: The total profit of a company after all expenses and taxes have been deducted from revenues.

NASDAQ Composite: A stock market index that includes almost all stocks listed on the NASDAQ stock exchange.

O

Open Interest: The total number of outstanding derivative contracts, such as options or futures, that have not been settled.

Option: A financial derivative that represents a contract sold by one party to another, offering the buyer the right, but not the obligation, to buy or sell a security at an agreed-upon price.

Over-the-Counter (OTC): The trading of securities directly between parties, as opposed to on an exchange.

P

P/E Ratio (Price to Earnings Ratio): A valuation measure comparing the current share price to its per-share earnings.

Payment Date: The date on which the dividend is actually paid to shareholders.

Penny Stock: A small company's stock that typically trades for less than $5 per share.

Portfolio: A collection of investments owned by an individual or institution.

Price-to-Book Ratio (P/B Ratio): A ratio used to compare a stock's market value to its book value.

Profit Margin: A measure of profitability calculated as net income divided by revenue.

Pullback: A temporary reversal in the price direction of a stock or asset, typically viewed as a short-term drop in an overall upward trend. Pullbacks provide opportunities for traders to buy at lower prices within a longer-term bullish trend.

Q

Quantitative Easing (QE): A monetary policy where a central bank buys securities from the market to increase the money supply and encourage lending and investment.

Quiet Period: The period of time when a company is legally restricted from promoting or discussing the upcoming IPO.

R

Record Date: The date by which shareholders must be on the company's books in order to receive the dividend payment.

Resistance: A stock price level at which a stock often stops rising because of a concentration of sellers.

Resistance Level: A price point at which a stock or market tends to face selling pressure.

Return on Equity (ROE): A measure of financial performance calculated by dividing net income by shareholders' equity.

Return on Investment (ROI): A measure of the profitability of an investment, calculated as the net profit divided by the initial cost of the investment.

Rights Issue: The offering of additional shares to existing shareholders at a discount to the current market price.

Risk: The potential for losing money on an investment.

S

S&P 500 (Standard & Poor's 500): A stock index of 500 of the largest and most widely-held public companies in the U.S.

Sector Rotation: An investment strategy involving the movement of money from one industry sector to another to capitalize on those sectors expected to perform well in the near term.

Securities and Exchange Commission (SEC): A U.S. federal agency responsible for enforcing federal securities laws and regulating the securities industry, including the stock and options exchanges. The SEC aims to protect investors, maintain fair and efficient markets, and facilitate capital formation.

Sell-Off: A rapid selling of securities, such as stocks or bonds, resulting in a decline in prices across a market or a particular security. Sell-offs can occur for various reasons including negative news, economic concerns, or investor panic.

Sharpe Ratio: A measure for calculating risk-adjusted return.

Short Selling: The sale of a security that the seller has borrowed with the intention of buying it back later at a lower price.

Spread: The difference between the bid price and the ask price of a security.

Stock: A type of security that signifies ownership in a

corporation and represents a claim on part of the corporation's assets and earnings.

Stock Buyback: A method by which a company purchases its own shares from the marketplace, reducing the number of outstanding shares.

Stock Split: An increase in the number of shares outstanding by issuing more shares to current shareholders.

T

Technical Analysis: A method of evaluating securities by analyzing statistics generated by market activity, such as past prices and volume. Unlike fundamental analysis, which focuses on the intrinsic value of a security, technical analysis aims to identify patterns and trends that can indicate future price movements.

Ticker Symbol: A unique series of letters assigned to a security for trading purposes.

Trading Volume: The number of shares or contracts traded in a security or an entire market during a given period.

Trailing P/E: Calculated using the past 12 months of earnings.

Trailing Stop: A type of stop order that moves with the market price.

Treasury Bond: A government debt security that earns interest until maturity, at which point the principal is paid back to the investor.

Turnover Ratio: A measure of the trading activity of a particular stock or portfolio.

U

Underperformance: When an investment's returns are lower than a benchmark or sector average.

Underwriter: A financial specialist who manages the public issuance and distribution of securities from a corporation.

Unicorn: A privately held startup company valued at over $1 billion.

V

Venture Capital: A type of private equity focused on early-stage, high-potential growth companies.

VIX (Volatility Index): An index that measures the market's expectation of future volatility, often referred to as the "fear gauge."

Volatility: A statistical measure of the dispersion of returns for a given security or market index.

Volume Weighted Average Price (VWAP): The average price of a security over a specified period, weighted by volume.

W

Wash Sale: A sale of a security at a loss and repurchase of the same or substantially identical security within 30 days, which IRS rules disallow for a tax deduction.

Watchlist: A list of securities that an investor monitors for potential trading opportunities.

Weighted Average Cost of Capital (WACC): A company's average cost of capital from all sources, including debt and equity.

X

X-Factor: An unexpected event or variable that can have a significant impact on the markets.

Y

Year-to-Date (YTD): A period starting from the beginning of the current year and continuing up to the present day.

Yield: The income return on an investment, such as the interest or dividends received, expressed as a percentage of the investment's cost or current market value.

Yield Curve: A line that plots the interest rates of bonds having equal credit quality but differing maturity dates.

Z

Zero-Based Budgeting: A budgeting method where all expenses must be justified for each new period.

Zero-Coupon Bond: A bond that is issued at a discount to its face value and does not pay interest.

Zombie Company: A firm that is unable to cover its debt servicing costs from current profits and can only repay outstanding debt through borrowing or asset sales.

Understanding these terms can provide you with a solid foundation for navigating the complexities of investing in the stock market.

REVIEW

Did you enjoy the read?
Have your people leave a review on Amazon in your words
letting me know if this book, or any of my self-help titles
were useful, or helped you in any way.

OTHER BOOKS BY

URBAN AINT DEAD

Tales 4rm Da Dale

The Hottest Summer Ever

Hittin' Licks For The Holidays: Atlanta

Wet Dreams On Lockdown: The Nurse

How To Publish A Book From Prison

By **Elijah R. Freeman**

Despite The Odds

By **Juhnell Morgan**

Good Girls Gone Rogue

Good Girls Gone Rogue 2

By **Manny Black**

Hittaz

Hittaz 2

Hittaz 3

Hittaz 4

Hittaz 5

Hittaz 6

Coldhearted

Coldhearted 2

By **Lou Garden Price, Sr.**

Charge It To The Game

Charge It To The Game 2

Charge It To The Game 3

A Summer To Remember With My Hitta

Snatched Up By A Hitta

Santa Sent Me A Real One For Christmas

Wet Dreams on Lockdown: The Unit Manager

Thug Me The Right Way 2

Thug Me The Right Way 3

Seizing A Gangsta's Heart For The Summer

Yours For The Taking

By **Nai**

A Setup For Revenge

A Setup For Revenge 2

Wet Dreams On Lockdown: The Librarian

By **Ashley Williams**

Trickin' on a Heaux for Christmas: A BBW Love Story

Homie Hoppin' For The Holidays

Wet Dreams on Lockdown: The Female C.O

Letters Of His Love

By **Telia Teanna**

The State's Witness

The State's Witness 2

The State's Witness 3

This Time Won't You Save Me

This Time Won't You Save Me 2

His Summer Side Piece

Holiday Heist

By **Kyiris Ashley**

Stuck In The Trenches

Stuck In The Trenches 2

By **Huff Tha Great**

Melted the Heart of a Menace

Wet Dreams On Lockdown: Lieutenant Grace

By **P. Wise**

Merry Trapmas: Ice & Frost

By **Mia Sky**

Thug Me The Right Way

By **DiamondATL & Nai**

COMING SOON FROM
URBAN AINT DEAD

The Hottest Summer Ever 2
THE G-CODE
Tales 4rm Da Dale 2
How To Build Your Credit From Prison
By **Elijah R. Freeman**

Good Girl Gone Rogue 3
By **Manny Black**

Despite The Odds 2
By **Juhnell Morgan**

Foreva Your Gangsta
By **Nai**

Coming Soon From

This Time Won't You Save Me 3
Healing The Heart Of A Detroit Gangsta
By **Kyiris Ashley**

Atlantastan 3
By **Chris Green**

IN The Streetz 5
By **Tron Hill**

BOOKS BY

URBAN AINT DEAD's C.E.O

<u>Elijah R. Freeman</u>

Triggadale

Triggadale 2

Triggadale 3

Tales 4rm Da Dale

The Hottest Summer Ever

Murda Was The Case

Murda Was The Case 2

Murda Was The Case 3

Hittin' Licks For The Holidays: Atlanta

Wet Dreams On Lockdown: The Nurse

How To Publish A Book From Prison

STAY CONNECTED

Follow
Elijah R. Freeman
On Social Media
FB: Elijah R. Freeman
IG: @the_future_of_urban_fiction

www.ingramcontent.com/pod-product-compliance
Lightning Source LLC
Chambersburg PA
CBHW060757120626
46557CB00001B/14